INTERACTIVE TECHNIQUES FOR THE ESL CLASSROOM

INTERACTIVE TECHNIQUES FOR THE ESL CLASSROOM

Connie L. Shoemaker

Associate Director
Spring International Language Center

F. Floyd Shoemaker

Regional Training Manager
Federal Emergency Management Agency

HEINLE & HEINLE PUBLISHERS
A Division of Wadsworth, Inc.
Boston, Massachusetts 02116

Director: Laurie E. Likoff
Production Coordinator: Cynthia Funkhouser
Cover Design: Caliber Design Planning
Compositor: Scientific Transcribers
Printer and Binder: McNaughton & Gunn

Interactive Techniques for the ESL Classroom

Library of Congress Cataloging in Publication Data

Shoemaker, Connie.
    Interactive techniques for the ESL classroom / Connie L.
Shoemaker, F. Floyd Shoemaker.
        p.   cm.
    Includes index.
    ISBN 0-8384-2671-9
    1. English language—Study and teaching—Foreign speakers.
2. English language—Problems, exercises, etc.   I. Shoemaker, F.
Floyd.   II. Title.
PE1128.A2S56   1991
428'.007—dc20   90-46708
                                                                                    CIP

94 93 92 91 9 8 7 6 5 4 3 2 1

To Mildred Grondahl Johnson for her creativity and skill with the English language

Preface

Interactive Techniques for the ESL Classroom is designed for the instructor of English as a second language or the student training to become an ESL teacher. It is a resource book of exercises grouped according to type: warm-ups and mixers, puzzles, competitive games, critical incidents, role plays, and simulations. These techniques, appropriate for beginning to advanced students, can enrich your existing curricular materials as introductions, as supplements, and as ways to review and reinforce. By using these exercises in your classes, you will add variety and interest and encourage students to express themselves in the target language.

Our combined ESL teaching and adult training experience has culminated in this collection of techniques. Some activities come directly from adult training; many started as training ideas and then were simplified and adapted to meet the requirements of the language classroom; others were personally developed by one of the authors in the ESL classroom in response to students' needs.

It is difficult to determine the source of many activities used in the classroom or training room. They are handed down from one instructor to another and frequently appear in published materials with no source identified. We have tried to supply bibliographic references for all exercises that can be linked to specific materials; others have been labeled "source unknown," and the remainder were designed by the authors.

Chapter 1 introduces recent research in adult education and demonstrates its link with current language learning research. Chapters 2 through 5 compile more than 80 exercises designed for immediate use in the classroom. Each exercise is organized by purposes, both affective and linguistic; level of English required; size of group; and materials needed. The procedure for using each exercise in the classroom is detailed in easy-to-follow steps. Variations are suggested following the exercise. These variations frequently include ways to follow up the exercise with writing or reading assignments. Where applicable, cultural notes are included. These explanations alert the instructor to students' cultural customs or rules that may necessitate adaptation of an exercise. The final chapter explores ways in which to adapt and create additional interactive exercises.

We encourage you to experiment with interactive techniques. Try some of them directly from the book; adapt others to fit your particular group of students; and, finally, use others as a pattern to create your own unique exercises. We believe they will stimulate your students' language learning and enrich your classrooms as they have ours.

Contents

1

Training Techniques Applied to Language Teaching

Adult training, a humanistic, learner-centered approach to the process of teaching, has been recognized by major corporations and innovative government agencies as a pathway to success. These organizations use adult training to develop knowledge and skills among their employees, to build group morale, to improve communication, and to facilitate healthy group functioning.

As a profession, adult training evolved during the 1960s when research and analysis of experience demonstrated that assumptions about children as learners may not be valid for adults as learners. In the past two decades, a model of human learning and techniques for facilitating learning, termed andragogy, has developed. Today, adult training has its own well-defined concepts, methods, and techniques. Although many of andragogy's concepts also are found in the theories of language learning, it is refreshing for the classroom teacher to examine the development of this new, but related, field.

Because training emphasizes the link between the world inside the classroom and the world outside, these criteria, methods, and techniques are readily applicable to the language classroom.

THE FOUR CRITERIA OF ADULT LEARNING

Professor Malcolm Knowles of Boston University identified four criteria that impact on the learning process of adults.[1]

Self-Concept of the Learner

Children conceive of themselves as dependent persons, but as they grow toward adulthood they experience a need for others to see them as being capable of self-direction. This change from a self-concept of dependency to one of autonomy is what we call psychological maturity or adult-

1

hood. Because of this self-concept, adults tend to resent being put into situations that violate their feelings of maturity, such as being talked down to, being judged, being treated with a lack of respect, or otherwise being treated like children.

When adults are faced with learning a new language, their mature self-concept is often in conflict with the fact that they have reverted, of necessity, to childlike language patterns. This makes it even more essential that language instructors treat these individuals as adults. When adults find that they are capable of self-direction in learning, they often experience a remarkable increase in motivation to learn and to continue the learning process on their own initiative. This discovery points out a major difference between assumptions of child learning, pedagogy, and adult learning. This difference exists in the relationship between teacher and learner and in the learner's concept of self with regard to the capacity for self-direction (Figure 1.1).

Dominant teacher   Dependent learner

Reciprocity in the teaching/learning transaction

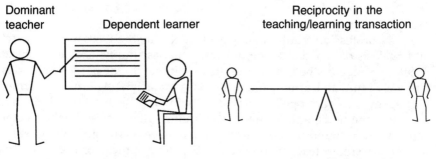

A Directing Relationship

A Helping Relationship

Figure 1.1

Utilizing the Learner's Experience

In the process of living, adults accumulate vast quantities of experience of differing kinds. It is safe to say that "we are our experience." Our experience is what we have done, i.e., the sum total of our life's impressions and our interaction with other persons and the world. "In the andragogical approach to education, the experience of adults is valued as a rich resource for learning."[2] Andragogy abounds with "experiential," two-way, and multidirectional techniques, such as group discussion, skill practice sessions, simulations, role playing, and team building. In this way, the experiences of all participants can be used as resources for learning. When individuals function as teachers and learners at the same time, using their experiences to facilitate the learning process, the second major difference between andragogy and pedagogy becomes clear (Figure 1.2).

One-way communication given by
teacher to learner

Multicommunication
shared by all

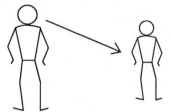

Experience of teacher valued as
primary resource for learning

Experience of all valued
as resources for learning

Figure 1.2

Readiness to Learn

As educators, we are familiar with the concept of "readiness to learn" or "teachable moment." It is widely known that educational development occurs best through a sequencing of learning activities into developmental tasks so that the learner is presented with opportunities for learning certain skills or topics when he or she is "ready" to assimilate them but not before. In this traditional, pedagogical approach, it is assumed that the teacher must take the total responsibility for designing the curriculum for the learners. While this may be true if the learners have no idea what they need to learn next, it has been shown that adults are capable of diagnosing their own needs for learning and designing learning activities around the specifics of their situation. "The facilitator of andragogical learning acts as a resource person to help the learners form interest groups and diagnose their learning needs."[3] In forming these groups, the instructor may provide some structure by suggesting the kinds of competencies needed to perform various roles or functions or the teacher may suggest several areas of interest into which learners may wish to group themselves to begin this diagnostic process (Figure 1.3).

Learners are grouped by grade and
class.

Learners group themselves according to
interests.

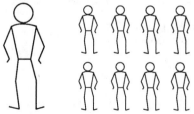

Teacher makes curriculum decisions
for learners.

Facilitator helps learners to diagnose
learning needs.

Figure 1.3

An example of this concept applied to the ESL classroom is the use of peer groups in writing. Students may form groups to aid each other in revision and editing or a group of students who share the same weakness, such as formation of thesis statements, may band together to work on recognizing focus statements. An additional example is found in a listening/ speaking situation in which students watch a video tape of three-minute speeches which they have presented. In watching the video, they try, with the help of the instructor, to pinpoint major grammatical mistakes. Then they work on grammar exercises specific to their grammatical weaknesses with a group of students sharing the same mistakes.

Time Perspective and Orientation to Learning

We are used to thinking of education in terms of "preparation for the future" rather than "doing in the present." When we were children, we were involved in the educational process of storing up information for use on some far-off day, following graduation. Our teachers presented us with information neatly packaged into subjects that we could unwrap as needed on our journey through life, and graduation seemed to be a sort of "rite of passage" from the learning world into the "doing world." In andragogical philosophy there is a strong impetus to close the gap between learning and doing. While adults are interested in planning and learning for the future, they seem to be more interested in learning for immediate application. Hence, learning in andragogical education is "problem centered" rather than "subject centered" (Figure 1.4).

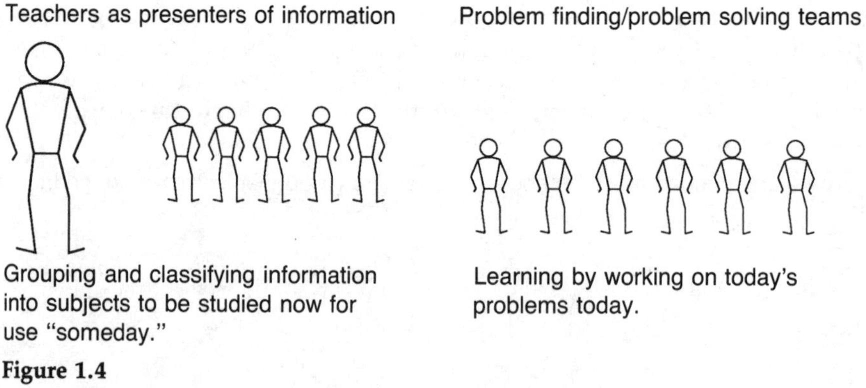

Teachers as presenters of information   Problem finding/problem solving teams

Grouping and classifying information   Learning by working on today's
into subjects to be studied now for   problems today.
use "someday."

Figure 1.4

The full meaning of andragogy, or self-directed learning, can be made clearer by comparing it with its opposite, pedagogy, which is teacher-directed learning. The word *pedagogy* is derived from the Greek words *paid* (meaning "child") and *agogus* (meaning "leader"). When we contrast the definitions of andragogy and pedagogy, this does not imply that children should be taught pedagogically and adults should be taught andragogically. "Rather, the two terms simply differentiate between two sets of assumptions about learners, and the teacher who makes one set of assumptions will teach pedagogically whether he or she is teaching children or adults, whereas the teacher who makes the other set of assumptions will teach andragogically whether the learners are children or adults," according to Knowles.[4] In fact, many of the innovations in schooling, such as open classrooms, nongraded schools, learning laboratories, community schools, and nontraditional study are based upon andragogical assumptions about children and youth as learners.

Perhaps what makes the difference between pedagogical and andragogical education is not so much the difference in the assumptions underlying their practice as in the attitude of the learners. If self-directed learners recognize that there are occasions on which they will need to be taught, they will enter those taught-learning situations in a searching, probing frame of mind and will exploit them as resources for learning without losing their self-directedness.

THE LINK BETWEEN ADULT LEARNING PHILOSOPHY AND THEORIES OF LANGUAGE LEARNING

At about the same time that adult training evolved, in the early 1960s, criticisms were being leveled against the then current audiolingual approach to language learning. These criticisms "focused on the overemphasis on tedious, mechanistic processes to which the student was not expected to make any spontaneous, personal contribution."[5] Noam Chomsky was the leader of this revolution in linguistic theory, flatly rejecting the prevalent reinforcement/reward theories of first language learning. Chomsky set forth his own theory that children are born with language learning abilities that take the form of a language acquisition device (LAD) that functions by making and testing hypotheses about the form of the grammar of the language.[6]

Natural Language Learning

Chomsky's theory led to the "natural language learning" approach, the basic principle of which is found in the much-discussed theory of second language acquisition (SLA) formulated by Stephen Krashen. According to Krashen and other SLA researchers, adult second language learners have two different ways of developing skills in a second language: learning and acquisition.[7] Language learning, which is a conscious process, is the product of either a formal language learning situation or a self-study program. It focuses students' attention on the form (structure) of the language. Acquisition, as opposed to learning, is a subconscious process similar to that by which children acquire their first language. Acquisition, according to Krashen, "appears to require, minimally, participation in natural communication situations. . . ."[8] It is precisely these "natural communication situations" that are created by the use of adult training techniques.

In the past, most language learning classrooms emphasized learning more than acquisition. Students listened to the teacher's lecture, took notes, and analyzed new structural items in the lesson. Later, they practiced providing correct answers either structurally or functionally but remained conscious of what they wanted to say. Then they were evaluated on their grammatical and lexical knowledge in a formal testing situation. However, in a natural communication situation, when students interact with speakers of their own language, they seldom focus their attention on the form of the language the speaker uses. Instead, they are concerned with what the speaker means or with the paralinguistic features of the speech (i.e., gestures, body language, etc.), which determine the quality of the message.

Krashen's Input Hypothesis

Another link between andragogy and language learning theory is found in Krashen's Input Hypothesis. In delineating this theory, Krashen states that people acquire languages by understanding messages—that is, by receiving what he calls "comprehensible input." Krashen believes the productive skills (speaking and writing) evolve from the receptive skills (listening and reading) and, consequently, should be given much more emphasis. A roughly tuned input, as opposed to a finely tuned input, is recommended. Roughly tuned input is the everyday conversation normally used in a native language, which includes all kinds of structures organized according to communicative needs. Finely tuned input is what goes on in the normal language classroom, where teachers select the language they use, not only simplifying their speech—which is natural—but in most cases using only the structures being analyzed at the moment. The advantages of using roughly tuned input are obvious: the language sounds more natural, students are exposed to a better kind of input, and structures will be previewed, then practiced, and finally, reviewed. The optimal input must be comprehensible, interesting and/or relevant, not grammatically sequenced, sufficient in quantity, and a little beyond the students' level of competence.[9]

Again, according to Krashen, understanding a message is not enough to assure language acquisition; one must be open to the message so that it reaches the LAD. Not all input reaches the LAD; somewhere along the way it is filtered and only part of it is acquired. This filtering process takes place in the affective filter, which acts like a gate controlling the amount of input. The affective filter "opens" or "closes" according to our mood. That is, if we are relaxed and in a pleasant learning environment, such as that emphasized in adult training, more input will reach the LAD, while if we feel tense or are in a negative environment, our efforts to provide input will be fruitless. That is why it is important to provide an appropriate acquisition environment in the classroom, eliminating anxiety and encouraging students, so they feel they really can acquire the language. Students are even encouraged just to listen to the language before speaking. Listening is usually accompanied by some form of activity, such as physical responses to instructions given in the target language, as in Asher's Total Physical Response.[10] When students begin to speak, activities typical of adult training, such as games, role play, problem-solving tasks, and sharing of experiences, are useful because the students focus on meaning rather than form.

Emphasis on Oral Output

For many language teachers, Krashen's second language acquisition theory has changed the concept of language teaching and has suggested new ideas for communicative techniques. There is also a growing recognition that students' oral output is instrumental in their acquisition of the new language. Terrell cites four reasons why it is important for beginning learners to speak as well as hear the new language: (1) By speaking to others, learners will provoke their conversation partners to generate the input they need for acquisition to take place. (2) By attempting to keep up their end of the conversation with a more fluent partner, learners provide the data necessary for their partners to gauge the appropriate input level. This enables partners to make their input comprehensible to the learner. (3) Conversation permits learners to test hypotheses they have formulated about how the language is put together and to receive feedback on the success of their attempts. (4) Speaking with natives or fluent nonnatives allows learners to match up their own output with that of others, thus helping them to form a realistic picture of their own developing communication skills.[11]

Influence of Affect-Based Approaches

Hand in hand with changes in the concept of language teaching in the 1970s came the influence of affect-based approaches, particularly humanistic psychology. The humanistic approach encouraged teachers to put students at ease in the classroom, emphasized the need to include vocabulary and activities for sharing values and expressing feelings and opinions, and stressed individual worth and differences in learning strategies. In addition, it addressed the questions of how we learn and who is responsible for learning. If all motivation is a result of internal need meeting and goal striving, then learning is internally motivated and the responsibility for learning lies within the learner.

The importance of working at the same time with feelings and intellect in group and individual learning was emphasized also by G. I. Brown in *Human Teaching for Human Learning: An Introduction to Confluent Education*.[12] The seven steps in the andragogical process given by Knowles are echoed in the four components of Confluent Learning, as described by Galyean: (1) learning in the present, utilizing the ongoing interests and energies of the class, (2) student-offered material as the basis for learning and practicing language structures, (3) interpersonal sharing and student-to-student communication, and (4) self-awareness and self-realization.[13] Activities based on these ideas provide for the cognitive, affective, and interactive aspects of learning. In this approach, the teacher becomes a nonauthoritarian facilitator who is open to sharing and growing in self-awareness with the students, traits which also were delineated by Charles Curran in his Counseling-Learning/Community Language Learning model.[14]

In this brief review of the communicative approach to teaching English as a second language, we can see links with the adult learning philosophy delineated by Knowles. The next step is to put these assumptions into practice in a classroom setting.

PUTTING PHILOSOPHY INTO PRACTICE

In his 1984 book *Andragogy in Action*, Malcolm Knowles makes seven suggestions for the trainer to keep in mind when designing an andragogical learning experience. The continuous, circular application of the seven steps may be viewed as a learning systems model that uses a "feedback loop"[15] (Figure 1.5).

The seven steps in the andragogical process have direct application to the ESL classroom.

Set the Learning Climate

This is one of the most important elements of the andragogical process. Knowles says that trainers, and teachers, need to create physical and psychological environments that are conducive to learning. Classrooms should be arranged to facilitate small-group interaction and to promote

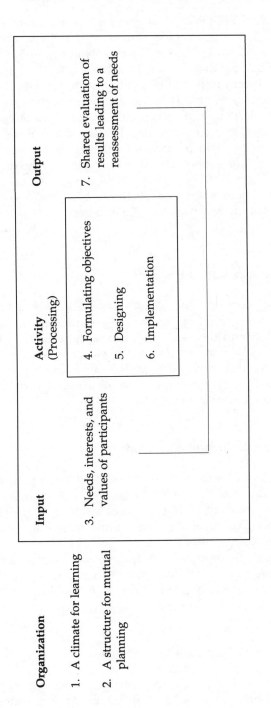

Figure 1.5 (*Source: A Trainer's Guide to Andragogy: Its Concepts, Experience and Application.* Washington, DC: U.S. Dept. of Health, Education and Welfare, 1973, p. 11.)

cheerfulness. The traditional classroom-lecture arrangement is too rigid, says Knowles. The psychological climate of the classroom should create mutual respect and trust. It should be open and supportive, and create an atmosphere of collaboration between teacher and student. Finally, learning should be fun. People bring with them to learning situations some feelings of anxiety and uncertainty. They need time to become acquainted with others in the situation and to have some experiences of accepting others and being accepted by them. This is the reason that Knowles recommends "warm-up" activities which often take the form of short games or fun experiences to set the proper climate among people who don't know each other.

The environment suggested by Knowles would allow the affective filter, as described by Krashen, to open and permit optimal input to reach the LAD.

Involve Learners in Mutual Planning

People don't commit to decisions if they have not had a role in making them. In the andragogical approach, trainers present several options for learning activities and then let the participants select the options. In the ESL classroom, students can also participate in choosing and planning activities with the teacher's guidance. Having an investment in what goes on in the classroom makes students of all ages eager to participate and gain the most benefit from the activities.

Involve Learners in Diagnosing Needs

Even if individuals have taken assessment tests, such as those used in language programs, they need to be involved in understanding and interpreting the results of such tests. Since learning is an internal process, those methods which involve the individual in self-directed inquiry will produce the greatest learning.

The best teachers perceive that the locus of responsibility for learning is in the learner, and thus they suppress their own compulsion to teach what they know students ought to learn in favor of helping students learn for themselves what they want to learn.

Involve Learners in Formulating Objectives

Translating needs into objectives requires moving from problem finding to problem solving. To achieve this goal, Knowles suggests making "learning contracts," a four-step process that translates learning needs into learning objectives; identifies resources to meet those objectives; specifies what evidence will be used to judge how well the objectives have been met; and determines how that evidence will be used for evaluation. His suggestion is similar to the notional/functional syllabus often used in ESL curricula.

Involve Learners in Designing and Carrying Out Plans

The fifth and sixth steps of the andragogical model combine to become the application phase. The design and implementation steps are seen as a subsystem of the total andragogical system; this means that all seven steps of the process are to be repeated again within these two steps. Knowles suggests that learners have input into the curriculum and into the ways in which the curriculum will be implemented. The trainer or teacher must avoid the temptation of designing the "content" of someone else's learning and concentrate instead on using his or her expertise to assist students in achieving their own learning goals.

Involve Learners in Evaluating Learning

The final step in the andragogical process requires participants to evaluate not only the achievement of their learning objectives, but also the quality and content of the training program or learning experience. Evaluation should be descriptive rather than judgmental because descriptive evaluation opens up joint exploration of needs for change and growth.

As we have reviewed the development of adult training techniques and their link with innovations in second language learning, a new view of the classroom and its students has emerged. The old authoritarian teacher facing straight rows of stationary desks has been replaced by an instructor who is in touch with the needs of his or her students: physiological needs for expression and movement, the need to feel secure in a caring group, the need for esteem for oneself and other students who contribute to the well-being of the total group, and, last, the need to discover not only who one is but also who one can become and what one can achieve in cooperation with others. The view of the new classroom also includes students busily working in small groups at activities they have helped choose and design. The students are interacting with each other, expressing feelings, describing experiences, giving opinions, listening actively, and assisting each other to complete tasks.

The chapters that follow offer a variety of activities designed to enhance students authentic use of English as a second language. The collection of exercises is an outgrowth of current trends in instruction, both in adult training and in second language learning. Chapter 2 features warm-ups and mixers that help students to become better acquainted and to build a feeling of membership in the group. Chapter 3 includes puzzles. This group of informal exercises requires students to develop solutions to situations by using the target language to share ideas, give directions, question possibilities, and respond to others' ideas. Chapter 4 focuses on games, which create a sense of fun and competition and stimulate natural and purposeful use of language. Role plays and critical incidents make up Chapter 5. These exercises emphasize real-life situations that require cultural understanding and use of English to resolve. Chapter 6 includes simulations, realistic but imaginary situations which a group must work through as a social unit. These exercises provide an opportunity for students to assume the identity of a native speaker involved and interacting with other native speakers in a specified setting. Chapter 7 offers guidelines and ideas for adapting and creating interactive techniques of your own.

NOTES

1. Malcolm Knowles. *The Modern Practice of Adult Education.* New York: Association Press, 1970.
2. *A Trainer's Guide to Andragogy: Its Concepts, Experience and Application.* Washington, DC: U.S. Dept. of Health, Education and Welfare, 1973 (HCFA 73-05301), p. 6.
3. *A Trainer's Guide,* p. 8.
4. Malcolm Knowles. *Self-Directed Learning.* Chicago: Follett, 1975, p. 19.
5. Wilga Rivers. *Communicating Naturally in a Second Language: Theory and Practice in Language Teaching.* New York: Cambridge University Press, 1983, p. 5.
6. Noam Chomsky. *Aspects of the Theory of Syntax.* Cambridge, MA: MIT Press, 1965, pp. 25–26.
7. Stephen D. Krashen. *Second Language Acquisition and Learning.* Oxford: Pergamon Press, 1981.
8. Stephen D. Krashen. *Principles and Practice in Second Language Acquisition.* Oxford: Pergamon Press, 1982, p. 10.
9. Stephen D. Krashen. *Principles,* p. 32.
10. James J. Asher. The Learning Strategy of the Total Physical Response: A Review. *Modern Language Journal* 50 (1966):79–84.
11. Tracy D. Terrell. The Natural Approach: An Update. *Modern Language Journal* 66 (1982):121–132.
12. George Isaac Brown. *Human Teaching for Human Learning: An Introduction to Confluent Education.* New York: Viking Press, 1971.

13. Beverly Galyean. A Confluent Design for Language Teaching. *TESOL Quarterly* 11 (1977):143–156.
14. Charles A. Curran. *Counseling-Learning in Second Languages.* Apple River, IL: Apple River Press, 1976.
15. Malcolm Knowles. *Andragogy in Action: Applying Modern Principles of Adult Learning.* San Francisco: Jossey Bass, 1984.

2

Warm-Ups and Mixers

The exercises in this chapter serve as "ice-breakers" or conversation starters. They help students to become better acquainted and to build a feeling of membership in the group, in addition to giving them practice in using the target language. All of the activities may be used during the first week of a new term, when a group of new students enters an already-established class, or at any point during a term simply as a means of reestablishing relationships among classmates.

Using warm-ups and mixers creates a classroom climate that is friendly and fun, a setting that has been encouraged by both adult trainers and researchers in second language learning.

EXERCISE 1: THAT WAS THE YEAR THAT WAS

Affective Purposes
To become acquainted with interesting events in the past lives of classmates

To stimulate curiosity about each other

Linguistic Purposes
To use the vocabulary of introductions

To practice the past tense

Levels   All levels except low beginning

Group Size   Total classroom, rotating to each individual

Materials   None

Procedure   Choose a year that fits the ages in the class. Ask students to introduce themselves (if they are not known to each other) and to tell where they were in this year, what they were doing, and what was the most important event of that year.

EXERCISE 2: LINE-UP—HOW LONG HAVE YOU BEEN HERE?

Affective Purposes
To become acquainted with classmates

To identify common experiences

Linguistic Purposes
To stimulate informal conversation

To practice the vocabulary of order, comparison

To practice questions/answers in present perfect

Levels   Beginning to intermediate

Group Size   Total class

Materials   None

Procedure
1. Announce the following to the class: "Think about how many years, months, days, or even hours you have been in the United States. When you have the length of time in mind, please line up in the front of the room, starting on my left, with the person who has been here the shortest time, and going to the right. In order to do this, you will have to ask each other, 'How long have you been in the U.S.?'"
2. After students have organized themselves, ask them to introduce themselves by telling how long they have been in the United States. This activity can be expanded to include comparisons between students and their partners on the right or left. For example: "My name is José. I've been in the U.S. for six months. I've been here longer than Latif." This comparison can become even more difficult if *who* clauses are added, such as "I have lived here longer than Latif, who has been here for only one month."

EXERCISE 3: LINE-UP—WHEN WERE YOU BORN?

Affective Purposes
To get students to mix with one another

To learn more about each other

Linguistic Purposes
To practice informal conversation

To practice *wh-* questions

To use forms of *to be born*

To practice *before, after*

Levels   All levels

Group Size   Total class

Materials   None

Procedure
1. Instruct students to recall the month and day on which they were born. Then follow the same procedure as in Exercise 2, but have students line up in order of the month and day they were born, beginning with January. Students will have to ask each other such questions as, "When were you born?" "Were you born before June 5?" "Were you born in January, too?"
2. When the class has organized itself in order of the calendar, have students introduce themselves and tell their birthdates. More advanced groups can add the city and country in which they were born. Another idea is to have students contrast their birthdates with the classmates on their left and right. For example, a student might say, "I'm Sylvie. I was born on February 5. I was born before Aubert but after Marie."

Variation   Another line-up similar to this might have students organize themselves according to age and then compare their age with students on either side. For example, "I'm Jean and I'm 21, two years younger than Maria." *Warning:* If you have a student who is much older or younger than the rest of the group, you may not want to choose this line-up because it may prove embarrassing.

EXERCISE 4: LINE-UP—YOUNGEST, OLDEST, OR IN-BETWEEN?

Affective Purposes
To share ideas and thoughts

To learn more about classmates

Linguistic Purposes
To practice vocabulary of order (*first, second*, etc.)

To use vocabulary of opinions (*I think. . ., I believe. . .*, etc.)

Levels   Intermediate through advanced

Group Size   Three groups consisting of 3–6 members each

Materials   None

Procedure
1. Ask the students to divide themselves into small groups according to their order of birth: first children, last children, and middle children. (For purposes of this exercise, middle children include all who are not first or last.)
2. When the groups have been formed, ask each group to discuss advantages and disadvantages they perceived in their lives as a result of their position in the family. One person in each group can be responsible for taking notes and reporting back to the class. After five minutes, ask groups to share their points of view.
3. This discussion is a good prewriting exercise to be followed by an assignment such as "What It Means To Be a First Child" (or middle or last child).

Variation   After students have divided into groups, have them list five adjectives that describe their personalities. Then ask them to share these with each other and to formulate a list of traits that they have in common as first, middle, or last children. This activity can be used as an idea starter for a composition or as a prereading activity to be followed by an article on birth order.

EXERCISE 5: TV INTERVIEWS

Affective Purposes
To facilitate becoming acquainted

To draw pairs of students closer together

Linguistic Purposes
To practice questions/responses

To practice superlatives

To practice information-getting skills (follow-up questions, asking for details, etc.)

Levels   Intermediate to advanced

Group Size   Dyads

Materials   None

Procedure
1. Have students choose a partner whom they do not know well. Allow 15–30 minutes for each pair to get acquainted and find out the other person's full name, country, biggest achievement in his or her life, most exciting adventure, biggest claim to fame (all As, most soccer goals, trips abroad, etc.), highest goal, best day of his or her life, most liked activity, favorite class in high school or college. In other words, try to find out what makes this person unique and special, what makes him or her worthy of a television interview. Suggest that students make notes while interviewing their subjects.
2. Have students prepare their interviews either as a homework assignment or in class. Suggest that they write a brief paragraph introducing their famous guest, TV-style. For example, "I would like to introduce our very important guest, Ali Awada, who has just arrived from Lebanon. I'm sure our TV audience will recognize Ali because he is well known as a star football player on the national team of his country. Ali, can you tell us about the most exciting game you ever played?" Also ask students to list several questions that they can ask their guests.
3. Place two chairs facing the class for the interviewer and guest. Have them take turns interviewing with a time limit of approximately five minutes for each interview. Students enjoy having these interviews videotaped or tape-recorded for later viewing.

Variation   Instead of a TV dialogue, students may interview their partners in order to write a short newspaper story featuring the most interesting and unique details about their new acquaintances.

EXERCISE 6: OPEN-ENDED INTERVIEWS

Affective Purposes
To become better acquainted

To become sensitive to another person's need for privacy

Linguistic Purposes
To practice asking and answering a variety of questions

To practice polite refusals (*I'm sorry, but I'd rather not answer that question, I don't think I want to answer that question, I'll pass on that question.*)

Levels   Advanced beginning to advanced

Group Size   Groups of 3–4 members each

Materials None

Procedure
1. Have the class break up into small groups (3–4 students).
2. Each of the groups should select one person to be the first interviewee. The other members of the group can ask any questions that they choose; however, the student being interviewed has the option to pass on any question.
3. At the end of a preset time limit (2–4 minutes), change roles and interview another group member until all have been interviewed.
4. After the interviews, have the group come together as a whole to discuss which kinds of questions were the easiest to answer and which were the most difficult.

EXERCISE 7: THE NAME GAME

Affective Purposes
To become familiar with names of classmates

To recognize similarities in naming traditions of various cultures

Linguistic Purposes
To correctly pronounce names of classmates

To increase vocabulary of introductions

Levels High beginning to advanced

Group Size Dyads

Materials None

Procedure
1. Have students pair up with someone of a different culture, if possible. Tell students that they are going to exchange information with their partners about their first and last names, so that they can introduce their partners to the class.
2. Students should answer the following questions for each other:
   a. What is your first name? (The interviewer should practice pronouncing the name.)
   b. Does this name have a special meaning?
   c. Are you named after someone in your family or your religion?
   d. What is your last name? (Again, the interviewer should learn correct pronunciation.)
   e. Does your family name have a special meaning? (Is it an occupation, a place name, the name of a characteristic? Does it tell where you are from?)

3. Have each pair stand in front of the class for introductions. Ask students being introduced to write their names on the chalkboard both in English and in their native languages. The introducer should say something like, "This is Melissa Grondahl. She is from Denmark. Her first name means "honey" and her last name is a place name that means "green valley."

EXERCISE 8: NONVERBAL INTRODUCTIONS

Affective Purposes
To become acquainted

To illustrate that interpersonal communication can be accomplished without words

Linguistic Purpose
To realize that gestures and other nonverbal methods play a role in communication

Levels   All levels

Group Size   Dyads

Materials Needed   None

Procedure
1. Tell students that the purpose of this exercise is to introduce oneself to his or her partner, but that this activity must be done without words. They may use gestures, signals, visuals, pictures, or anything nonverbal. The instructor may offer hints, such as pointing to a wedding ring to indicate marriage, an in-place running movement to indicate the hobby of jogging, or the like (2–3 minutes each).
2. Students should test their understanding of nonverbal cues by verbally introducing their acquaintances to the class.

EXERCISE 9: UNFINISHED SENTENCES

Affective Purposes
To become better acquainted

To share attitudes, beliefs, and interests

Linguistic Purpose
To practice writing and conversing using a variety of sentence structures, including the conditional and superlative.

Levels Intermediate to advanced

Group Size Triads

Materials Unfinished sentences handout

Procedure
1. Give students the handout that follows and ask them to complete the sentences.
2. Break up into groups of three to share completed sentences and to determine answers that are the same, answers that are very unusual, and answers that are the most interesting.
3. Have each group share with the class the most common answer, the most unusual answer, and the most interesting answer.

Unfinished Sentences Handout

1. On Saturdays, I like to . . .
2. If I had only 24 hours to live, I would . . .
3. If I could buy the car of my choice, I would choose . . .
4. I feel best when people . . .
5. If I had a million dollars, I would . . .
6. Secretly I wish . . .
7. If I could change the world, I would . . .
8. Right now the most important thing in my life is . . .
9. If I could visit any place in the world, I would go to . . .
10. The most exciting thing I have done is . . .

EXERCISE 10: JIGSAW PUZZLES

Affective Purpose
To cooperate with classmates in a team situation

Linguistic Purpose
To practice the target language in an informal situation with a common purpose

Levels All levels

Group Size   Four groups of 3–5 members each

Materials   Four different 10- to 20-piece jigsaw puzzles

Procedure
1. Divide the class into four teams. Explain to the teams that their purpose is to sort out and put together the pieces of their puzzle. They are to use English to make suggestions, give directions, ask for specific puzzle pieces, and so on, in order to complete their puzzle first.
2. Give each member of every team one piece of the puzzle assigned to that team. Place all remaining pieces of the four puzzles together on a table and mix thoroughly.
3. Ask one member of each team to come to the table to select one piece of their puzzle. That team member returns to the group which, in turn, tries to assemble the pieces.
4. Ask another member of each team to come to the table to select another piece. Continue this procedure until one group signals completion of its puzzle.

EXERCISE 11: INTEREST TAGS

Affective Purposes
To learn about classmates' interests

To build a cohesive group

Linguistic Purposes
To use descriptive words

To practice asking questions to find out details

Levels   All levels

Group Size   Total class

Materials   5″ × 7″ index cards, thin felt-tip markers, straight pins

Procedure
1. Give each student a 5″ × 7″ index card, a marker, and a straight pin.
2. Ask students to write their first names on the fronts of the cards with a marker in large letters, so they will be visible across the room. Then ask them each to write five or six words that tell something about themselves, for example, *guitar, tennis, travel, fun-loving, jazz*. These words also should be written on the front of the card in large letters.

3. Encourage students to pin on their cards and to circulate around the room reading other student's name tags and asking questions.
4. One of several "windups" may complete this exercise:
   a. Students may introduce themselves, explaining in more detail what their interests are.
   b. Each student may try to find a partner who shares one of his or her interests. The partners will introduce each other with details of the shared interest.
   c. The teacher may "quiz" students on what they remember about each other. For example, "Which student likes to listen to jazz music?"

EXERCISE 12: DESIGN A T-SHIRT

Affective Purposes
To share personal preferences with a partner

To form class friendships

To use art and language to express oneself

Linguistic Purposes
To focus on most important ideas about a person

To practice information-gathering skills

Levels   All levels

Group Size   Dyads

Materials   T-shirt handout (Figure 2.1) and felt-tip markers

Procedure
1. Ask class members to pair off with someone they do not know well.
2. Instruct them to spend 4–5 minutes talking with their partners. During this time they should ask each other about
   a. A favorite color
   b. A favorite animal
   c. A famous person they admire
   d. A song they like
   e. A favorite food
   f. A favorite proverb or saying
3. When the time is up, ask each student to design a T-shirt for the person he or she interviewed. Students should focus only on the most important or interesting characteristics of the person since not all details will fit on one shirt. In other words, they must focus on what is important or

Figure 2.1 T-shirt handout.

unique about the student. The design should be sketched on the T-shirt handout with colored felt-tip markers.
4. After the T-shirts are completed, ask students to share their designs with the class.

EXERCISE 13: NEW AND GOOD

Affective Purposes
To energize the group

To share positively with each other

Linguistic Purposes
To practice describing an event

To use the vocabulary of feelings

Levels   All levels

Group Size   Groups of 3–5 students each

Materials   None

Procedure
1. Divide into groups (3–5 students).
2. Ask group members to share something "new and good" that happened to them within the last week. This is a voluntary response exercise, so you may suggest that students do this in any order. (Examples might include: "I'm proud of myself because I took the bus for the first time and didn't get lost," or "I made an American friend in the cafeteria.")
3. Encourage other group members to respond positively after each student contributes or to ask questions about the positive event described.

EXERCISE 14: INTERNATIONAL BINGO

Affective Purposes
To become better acquainted with members of a group

To include a wide range of individuals in a trusting and accepting group interaction

Linguistic Purpose
To practice asking questions in all forms

Levels   All levels

Group Size   10–200 people

Materials   Bingo cards and pencils

Procedures   This exercise has been used effectively with groups of ESL students, with instructors, and with a mixed group of students, host families, and instructors. The key to success is in adaptation of the bingo card to fit the members of the group. (See the example in Figure 2.2.)

1. Distribute International Bingo cards to all participants.
2. Tell the group that the object of this game is to get acquainted with as many people as possible in a short time by completing all the squares on the bingo card.
3. In order to complete a square, you must find a person who fits the

Someone who speaks three languages.	A girl with blue eyes.	Someone who has lived in Bangkok.	Someone who likes lollipops.	Someone who likes Michael Jackson's voice.
Someone who knows how to dance the salsa.	Someone who likes jazz music	An American who drives a Japanese car.	Someone with only one brother.	A student whose father is a businessman.
Someone who plays a musical instrument.	An American who plans to be a teacher of small children.	F R E E	A student who has been in the U.S. for more than one year.	A student who has been in the U.S. for less than three months.
Someone who comes from a country that has a lot of oil.	Someone who has studied tae kwon do.	An engineering student.	Someone who has more that two pets at home.	Someone who has an April birthday.
Someone who has studied dance.	Someone who is traveling to another country this summer.	A student who likes to play or watch basketball.	A soccer (football) player.	Someone whose favorite color is blue.

Figure 2.2   International Bingo card.

description in that square of the bingo card. For example, one square asks for someone who speaks three languages. When you locate a person who speaks three languages, have him or her initial the square. Note: If the group is large, emphasize the rule that a person can initial only one square. If the group has fewer than 25 people, allow players to initial more than one square.

4. Tell participants that the first person to complete a card should shout "Bingo!"

EXERCISE 15: WHO AM I?

Affective Purposes

To allow students to become acquainted quickly in a nonthreatening way

To share important facts about each other

Linguistic Purposes

To use all verb tenses

To practice vocabulary of life stages and events

Levels   Intermediate to advanced

Group Size   Total class

Materials   8½" × 11" sheets of paper to be used as name tags, felt-tip markers

Procedure

1. Students receive materials and are allowed 10 minutes to draw a "life line," a graph of their lives to the present, showing high points or, if they wish, a projected life line which includes their future hopes, indicating where they are now. An example is shown in Figure 2.3.
2. Students circulate around the room to look at each other's charts. At this time, they do not speak to each other.
3. Ask participants to return to a person they think would be interesting to speak to. Allow two minutes for questions and conversation and then ask students to move on to the next "interesting person."
4. Life lines can be posted on the wall, so students can become better acquainted.

Variations   (1) Students may draw a picture or pictures of themselves, a caricature, a cartoon strip, or the like. (2) Students may draw a pie with different-sized wedges to illustrate percentages of themselves devoted to

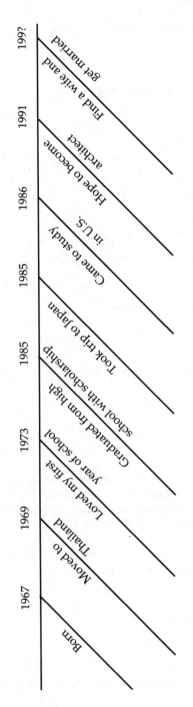

Figure 2.3   Sample life line.

certain life focuses, for example, studying, friends, music, travel, and so on. (3) Students may draw pictures of animals, objects, or music with which they identify.

EXERCISE 16: MY HOMETOWN

Affective Purposes
> To break the ice
>
> To allow students to discover similarities between themselves and other students
>
> To become better acquainted

Linguistic Purposes
> To use simple present tense
>
> To use vocabulary of directions
>
> To use descriptive words related to size, location, appearance

Levels   Beginning to advanced

Group Size   Total class

Materials   A large world map, sticky labels (or labels and straight pins), felt-tip markers

Procedure
1. Post the map in the classroom. Ask students to make labels with their names, the names of their hometowns, and the names of their countries.
2. As students place their labels on the map, have each briefly describe his or her hometown in terms of location in the country, approximate size, interesting features of the town, favorite places to go, location of their house or apartment, and so on.

Variations   Have students draw maps of their hometowns to show to the class while they describe the towns.

EXERCISE 17: DINNER PARTY

Affective Purposes
> To allow students to share experiences in a nonthreatening manner
>
> To promote acquaintance and a feeling of interaction in a new group

Linguistic Purposes
To give brief impromptu speeches

To use all verb tenses

Levels Beginning to advanced

Group Size Total class

Materials One Dinner Party booklet for each student

Procedure
1. Prepare a Dinner Party booklet for each participant. The booklet should be assembled so that only one page can be read at a time.
2. Instruct students to arrange themselves in two lines of chairs facing each other with a comfortable distance between them, as though they were seated across a long table. If there is an odd number of participants, one person takes the place as "head of the table."
3. Give a Dinner Party booklet to each student. Tell the students that the activity includes a series of paired conversations. Each pair will discuss one topic (one page of the booklet) for two minutes. Then each person will move one place to the left, turn the page, and share the next topic with a new partner. As the activity progresses, students will face partners they already have talked to. At this point, instruct them to move to a new partner. The activity will continue until each person has shared with every other person. If there is an uneven number of participants, explain that the person at the head of the table is the timekeeper, who announces when it is time for participants to move to the next partner and the next topic. If there is an even number, the teacher is timekeeper.
4. Tell students to open their booklets to page 1 and to begin the first round of sharing. Call time for each round (or have the head of the table call time), and instruct students to move on to the next topic.

Dinner Party Booklet

Instructions With each new partner, turn to a new page in this booklet and take turns sharing the topic printed there. Do not skip pages. Do not look ahead in this booklet.

Page 1:   One of my favorite times of the year is . . .

Page 2:   One of my best memories of childhood is . . .

Page 3:   A place I would like to visit is . . .

Page 4:   I am really looking forward to the time when I . . .

Page 5:   What I remember most about my closest childhood friend is . . .

Page 6:   I came to this school because . . .

Page 7:   Three things I think I am really good at are . . .

Page 8:   One thing about me that I would like to change is . . .

Page 9:   Pick a topic from the last three pages and ask your partner to tell you his or her answer to it.

Page 10:   What I miss most about my country is . . .

Page 11:   What I like most about this country is . . .

Page 12:   My favorite food is . . . because . . .

Page 13:   When I am ten years older, I would like to be . . .

Page 14:   When I find time to be alone, I like to . . .

Page 15:   My favorite TV program is . . .

Page 16:   One of the hardest times in my life was . . .

Page 17:   One of the most interesting times in my life was . . .

Page 18:   A person I really admire is . . .

Source Adapted from J. William Pfeiffer and John E. Jones (eds.). *A Handbook of Structured Experiences for Human Relations Training*, Vol. VII. San Diego: University Associates, 1979, pp. 5–10. Used with permission.

EXERCISE 18: BIRTH SIGNS

Affective Purposes
To develop a feeling of camaraderie

To discover similar interests and characteristics among classmates

Linguistic Purposes
To practice asking and answering questions

To use the vocabulary of similarities and differences

To use simple present tense

Levels All levels

Group Size   Total group

Materials   A poster or sign for each birth-sign group, as follows:

1. Aries, the Ram (March 21–April 19)
2. Taurus, the Bull (April 20–May 20)
3. Gemini, the Twins (May 21–June 20)
4. Cancer, the Crab (June 21–July 22)
5. Leo, the Lion (July 23–August 22)
6. Virgo, the Virgin (August 23–September 23)
7. Libra, the Balance Scales (September 24–October 23)
8. Scorpio, the Scorpion (October 24–November 21)
9. Sagittarius, the Archer (November 22–December 21)
10. Capricorn, the Goat (December 22–January 19)
11. Aquarius, the Water Bearer (January 20–February 18)
12. Pisces, the Fish (February 19–March 20)

Procedure
1. Instruct students to look for the sign that represents their birth date and to form a group with other students at the sign. (If the total group is small, form subgroups according to clusters of birth signs: spring, summer, fall, and winter, or earth, air, fire, and water).
2. Ask the members of each group to share information with each other to find out what they have in common and to prepare a one-minute report for the class.
3. Have each group report back to the class on their common traits.
4. The discussion can be continued with the following questions: What are horoscopes? Do newspapers in your country have horoscopes each day? Do you believe in them? Why are people interested in finding out their "future" or predictions for the day?

Variation   To each poster, attach a description of the common characteristics of persons with that sign. Have students compare their characteristics with the description to determine if they "fit."

EXERCISE 19: EXCHANGE TAGS

Affective Purposes
   To develop an atmosphere conducive to group interaction

   To enjoy getting acquainted

Linguistic Purposes
   To practice listening skills

To use first- and third-person pronouns with present tense verbs

To use reported speech

Levels   Intermediate to advanced

Group Size   Total class

Materials   Name tags that can be pinned on participants

Procedure
1. Introduce the activity as a get-acquainted exercise that will offer students listening and speaking practice.
2. Give students name tags and ask them to print their names and pin on the tags.
3. Direct participants to introduce themselves to someone in the class whom they do not know. Then ask them to exchange information about themselves for two minutes.
4. Call time and ask students to exchange name tags with the person they have been talking to and then go on to meet another student. Each student will talk about the person whose name tag they are wearing. For example, a student wearing Jorge's tag might say, "I'd like to tell you about Jorge. He's from Venezuela. He told me that he has six brothers." His partner might respond, "Li Lei is from China. She plays the piano and will study music."
5. Call time again and have participants switch name tags and find others to talk to about the person whose name tag they are wearing. Continue this process until most or all of the participants have had a chance to talk to each other.
6. Have students find their own name tags and wear them.
7. Ask students to debrief the activity by sharing interesting facts they found out about their classmates.

EXERCISE 20: INNER CIRCLE

Affective Purposes
To become better acquainted with classmates

To share common events in students' lives

Linguistic Purposes
To give detailed personal information in response to questions

To practice simple present, present perfect

Levels   All levels

Group Size   Total class

Materials   None

Procedure
1. Seat students in a circle. Explain the purpose of the exercise, which is to become better acquainted with each other and to practice answering personal questions with details. Tell them that you will read a question. If they can answer "yes" to that question, they should stand in the center of the circle and give students details about their answer. For example, the teacher asks, "Who has more than three children in their family?" Shen and Maria stand in the circle. Shen explains, "My family has six children. The youngest is three months and the oldest is 16. Four are boys and two are girls." Maria says, "I have four children in my family. I'm the oldest and we're all girls."
2. Some suggested questions include:
   a. Who has traveled to the United States before?
   b. Who wants to study engineering after finishing English?
   c. Who speaks three or more languages?
   d. Who has one or more brothers?
   e. Who has more than two sisters?
   f. Who has traveled to more than two countries?
   g. Who lives in a capital city?
   h. Who knows how to play a musical instrument?
   i. Who has studied in a university?
   j. Who likes to play basketball?
   k. Who likes to draw or paint?
   l. Who has played on a soccer team?
   m. Who likes jazz music?
   n. Who plans to study business at college or a university?
   o. Who has been lost in this town?
3. Have students sit down in the circle of chairs after each question.

Puzzles

The informality of this next group of exercises, puzzles, heightens interest and communicative energy and lowers anxiety and inhibitions about speaking English. When puzzles are presented to a group, students are required to develop solutions to the situations given them. These solutions come about through using English to share ideas, to give directions, to question possibilities, to respond to others' ideas, and so on.

Puzzles frequently are used in adult training as group builders. In the ESL classroom they can be used to unify a group and in many other ways: to rejuvenate a class when attention is lagging, to encourage a pair or a group to work together toward a solution, as a warm-up preceding another classroom activity, as a prewriting exercise which would be followed by writing clear directions for a solution, and to point out the importance of a particular approach to working through a task.

EXERCISE 1: HOW MANY SQUARES?

Affective Purpose
To use a systematic approach to work through a complex task

Linguistic Purposes
To describe a system in detail

To use chronological order to describe a process

To use cardinal numbers

Levels All levels

Group Size Dyads

Materials How Many Squares handout

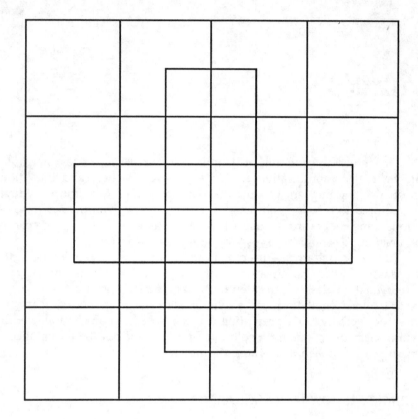

Figure 3.1   How Many Squares handout.

Procedure

1. Ask each dyad to count the number of squares in the How Many Squares handout (Figure 3.1). Suggest that they ask each other questions, make suggestions, and, in general, use each other's ideas to solve the puzzle. The team closest to the correct number wins.
2. Ask each dyad to describe its counting system. Did you have a systematic approach (a way of solving the problem step-by-step) when you counted your squares? Did it help to have a system?

Answer   There are at least 163 squares in the puzzle.

Variation   Base a writing assignment on the puzzle solution. Have students describe the process of completing this task or have them write about the importance of solving problems systematically.

EXERCISE 2: THE SPY IN THE BLACK TRENCH COAT

Affective Purposes
To promote cooperative problem solving

To have fun

Linguistic Purposes
To use the vocabulary of problem solving

To practice using prepositions of position, such as *in front of*, *next to*, and *to the left*

To practice conditionals (*if* clauses)

Levels   Intermediate to advanced

Group Size   Triads

Materials   Spy in the Black Trench Coat handout

Procedure
1. Tell the class that they are going to solve a puzzle by working in groups of three students each. Give each student a handout and, if necessary, briefly discuss unfamiliar vocabulary, such as *trench coat, khaki, arrangement, stared*.
2. After dividing the class into triads, instruct each group to find out who is the spy in the black trench coat by discussing each of the 12 facts. Suggest that they make notes on the picture in the handout as they discover who each of the spies is.
3. The group that finishes first must tell how they solved the puzzle and answer any questions that others may have.

The Spy in the Black Trench Coat Handout

1. Four spies in trench coats sat in four facing seats.
2. As they traveled the Peking Express.
3. With two by the window and two by the aisle.
4. The arrangement was strange (as you guessed).
5. The English spy sat on Mr. B's left.
6. Mr. A had a coat colored tan.
7. The spy dressed in olive was on the German spy's right.
8. Mr. C was the only cigar-smoking man.
9. Mr. D was across from the American spy.

10. The Russian, in khaki, had a scarf round his throat.
11. The English spy stared out the window on his left.
12. So who was the spy in the black trench coat?

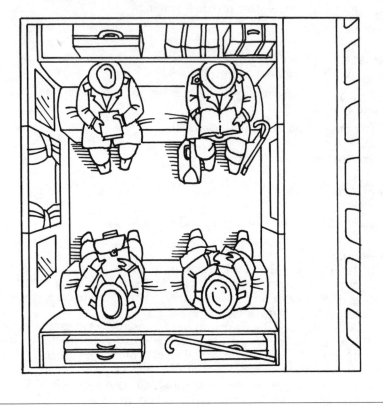

Answer   The spy in black is the one in the lower left corner of the picture.

Explanation of the Solution   The English spy is the one with Mr. B on his right (line 5) and the window on his left (line 11). The spy in the olive coat is to the right of the German (line 7), so the German must be sitting in the other aisle seat, across from Mr. B. The Russian is in khaki (line 10), so he can't be the man in olive by the window but must be Mr. B. By elimination, the man with the olive coat is American and the Englishman across from him is Mr. D. (line 9). Mr. A is wearing a tan coat (line 6), so he must be the German. By a process of elimination, Mr. C is the American spy, and it is the Englishman who has the black trench coat. In other words,

MR. C.	MR. A.	MR. D.	MR. B.
American	German	English	Russian
Olive Coat	Tan Coat	Black Coat	Khaki Coat

Source Adapted from S. Bianchi, J. Butler, and D. Richey. *Warmups for Meeting Leaders.* San Diego: University Associates, 1990, pp. 76–77. Used with permission.

EXERCISE 3: CONNECT THE DOTS

Affective Purpose
To use imagination by going beyond preconceived notions

Linguistic Purposes
To practice the vocabulary of directions (*vertical, horizontal, diagonal, left, right, up, down,* etc.)

To describe a process using chronological order vocabulary (*first, second, after, then,* etc.)

To use the imperative (*go, draw, make,* etc.)

Levels Intermediate to advanced

Group Size Individuals or triads

Materials Connect the Dots handout

Procedure
1. Give each student or group the Connect the Dots handout (Figure 3.2, top) and emphasize these instructions: Connect all nine dots using four straight lines, each connected to the other. In other words, do not lift your pencil. The first and last line may either start or end without being connected to anything.
2. After five minutes, ask if anyone has completed the task. If not, give the hint that it is necessary to go outside the square in order to solve the puzzle. If someone is now able to solve the puzzle, have that person give verbal instructions while you complete the puzzle on the chalkboard. If no one is able to solve the puzzle, have students follow your detailed verbal instructions to solve it (Figure 3.2, bottom).

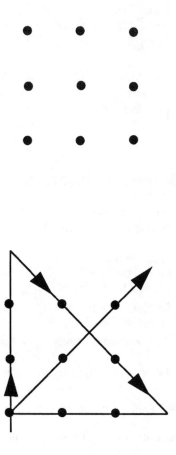

Figure 3.2   Top: Connect the Dots handout. Bottom: Solution to Connect the Dots.

Variation   Have students write a short process composition that gives details of how to solve the Connect the Dots puzzle. Suggest that they begin with a focus statement that expresses their attitude about the particular task. (Is it simple? Does it require a special skill or perception?) Then suggest they give specific details of the solution, using introductory phrases to mark the steps (first, second, then, etc.). A concluding sentence might state what the finished puzzle looks like.

This puzzle and those that follow may also be assigned as homework for the individual student. Class time can then be used to discuss solutions and to do follow-up activities.

EXERCISE 4: MORE DOTS

Affective Purpose
To apply imagination and previous experience to a more difficult puzzle

Linguistic Purposes
To practice the vocabulary of directions

To describe a process

To use the imperative verb form (*draw, go, move, connect,* etc.)

Levels Intermediate to advanced

Group Size Individuals or triads

Materials More Dots handout

Procedure
1. Give each student a More Dots handout (Figure 3.3, top) and explain that in this exercise there are 16 dots that must be connected using six straight lines, each connected to the other. The first and last lines may either start or end without being connected to anything.
2. After 5–10 minutes, ask if anyone has completed the puzzle. If someone is able to solve the puzzle, have that person give verbal instructions while a student or the instructor follows instructions on the chalkboard (Figure 3.3, bottom). Continue with instructions as in Exercise 3.

EXERCISE 5: TELL ME HOW, PLEASE!

Affective Purpose
To cooperate on a task that involves giving and following directions

Linguistic Purposes
To give detailed directions

To listen carefully and follow directions

To practice vocabulary of shapes, sizes

To use imperative verbs (*draw, make, put,* etc.)

To use prepositions of place (*next to, inside, outside, to the right,* etc.)

Levels High beginning to advanced

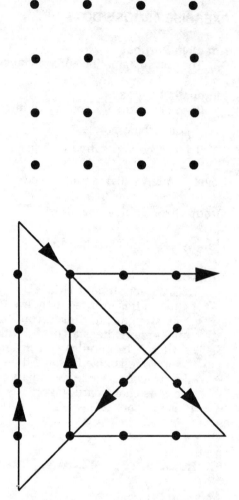

Figure 3.3   Top: More Dots handout.
Bottom: Solution to More Dots.

Group Size   One volunteer and remainder of class

Materials   One handout for volunteer, pencils and paper for class members

Procedure
1. Ask for a volunteer from the group. The volunteer will give instructions to the class members on how to draw a diagram (Figure 3.4) which the group cannot see. Give the volunteer the diagram to study for a few minutes. Allow the volunteer to ask questions about necessary vocabulary.
2. Instruct the group to draw the diagram just as it is described by the volunteer. Emphasize that the volunteer must use only words, no gestures. Participants are not allowed to ask questions.

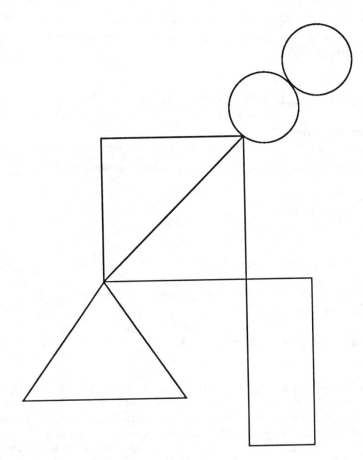

Figure 3.4 Sample diagram.

3. When instructions are complete, have the participants compare their drawings with the handout. If there is a wide variation in drawings, discuss the specific language that would have clarified the instructions.
4. Try again with a new volunteer and a new diagram.

Variations (1) Small groups (3–5 students) may be used, with one volunteer from each group giving instructions. Students can be paired and seated back-to-back. In this variation, one student is the sender of information and the other is the receiver. The sender describes the diagram or picture in the handout and the receiver draws it according to the sender's instructions. The receiver is not permitted to ask questions, laugh, sigh, or in any other way communicate information. This variation can lead into a discussion of how nonverbal language adds to our understanding of a language.

(2) A picture, an object, or a simplified diagram can be used. (3) This exercise can be used as a warm-up for a writing assignment that emphasizes clear, specific language.

EXERCISE 6: PRECONCEIVED NOTION

Affective Purposes
To demonstrate how a "mind-set" can block communication

To open minds for a discussion of cultural stereotypes

Linguistic Purposes
To express opinions

To use *before* and *after*

Levels   Intermediate to advanced

Group size   Total class for initial exercise, groups of 3–4 students each for discussion of stereotypes

Materials   Preconceived Notion handout

Procedure
1. After everyone has received a handout (Figure 3.5), give the class the following directions: "Keep the arrow pointing down. If you can read what is on the page, please raise your hand. Don't tell anyone else." Check student response and continue. "Okay, two of you know what it says. Here is a hint for the rest of the class. Try looking at the white space rather than the black markings. Now what do you see? That's right; the word is 'FLY'."
2. What made it difficult to read the word? (We expected to see the word printed in black.)
3. Have you ever had other experiences with expecting something to be a certain way, but it turned out to be different and it was difficult for you to "see" that difference? (Give students an opportunity to suggest expectations of what the United States would be like, preconceived ideas of Americans, etc.) Don't allow discussion to go for more than a few minutes because the remainder of time should be spent discussing additional questions in small groups.) You may also wish to discuss the meaning of "mind-set" and "preconceived notion."
4. Tell students that they are going to divide into small groups (3–4 students) to discuss how a "mind-set" can block our enjoyment of an experience or can stop us from communicating with others. Each group should discuss the following questions:
   a. What ideas did you have about the United States before leaving your country?
   b. Where did you get these ideas?
   c. Were these ideas correct? Were any of them wrong? Which ones?

Figure 3.5 Preconceived Notion handout.

   d. Did having the wrong idea about something make your adjustment to the United States more difficult? Why or why not?

   e. What wrong ideas do you think people might have about your culture or your country?

   f. If you met someone who had a wrong idea about your culture, how would it affect your getting acquainted and talking to each other?

Variation   This exercise can be followed by a composition assignment, such as: My First Ideas about the United States, How My Ideas about the United States Have Changed, Stereotypes of Americans, Stereotypes of My Country, or An Open Mind Helps Cultural Adjustment.

EXERCISE 7: READING JIGSAWS

Affective Purposes
   To work together as a group on a common task

   To develop an approach for problem solving

Linguistic Purposes
   To integrate skills of communication and meaning

   To use both holistic and sequential processes of reading comprehension

   To use grammar and punctuation cues to interpret meaning

Levels   All levels

Group Size   Dyads

Materials   A text that relates to the knowledge, interest, and level of the students. The text should be typed double spaced, mounted on cardboard, and cut into segments at meaning boundaries. The pieces should then be shuffled and put into an envelope labeled with the topic of the reading. The teacher should keep a card on which the entire reading passage is typed.

Procedure   Divide the class into pairs. Give each pair an envelope. Tell students that the pieces of the reading will fit together exactly to form an account of the topic listed on the envelope. Students should follow these steps:

1. Lay pieces on a desk or table one by one so they can be read easily. (Explain to students that some words and phrases may be unfamiliar, but that should not stop them from putting the text together.)
2. After scanning the pieces, choose the title and place it at the top of a clear space on the desk or table.
3. Put together the text piece by piece until it makes sense.
4. When satisfied with the meaning, ask the teacher for the card with the complete text to compare it for accuracy.

5. Make corrections, if necessary, and reread.
6. A possible final step would be to have the student write out the passage from memory to be compared to the check card.

Example of Reading Jigsaw (For intermediate to advanced group. Slash marks indicate where text should be cut.)

Earth Day Looks at Planet's Problems

Earth day, which was celebrated in the United States in 1990,/ pointed out four worldwide concerns:/ disappearing forests,/ rising temperatures,/ holes in the ozone,/ and acid rain./
Some scientists believe that cutting down tropical rain forests/ in other parts of the world/ may affect the weather in this country./ Tropical rain forests,/ which are the home to many animals and plants,/ are being cut down for wood and farming land./
Scientists also are calling attention/ to the "greenhouse effect."/ The buildup of certain gases,/ such as carbon dioxide,/ in the atmosphere/ may act like the top of a greenhouse./ A problem results when the heat close to the earth/ is unable to escape/ into space like it used to./
A third concern is the damage to the ozone layer/ which has been caused by use of technology/ such as fire extinguishers and air conditioning coolants./
The final problem/ results when some air pollutants/ in the atmosphere mix with the sunlight./ They form an acid which falls back to Earth/ in the form of snow, rain, or hail./ Thus, acid rain creates acid water/ in lakes and kills fish.

Note: The envelope should be marked: "Earth Day"

EXERCISE 8: OUTLINE JIGSAWS

Affective Purposes
To work together as a group on a logical task

To develop an approach for problem solving

Linguistic Purposes
To integrate skills of communication and meaning

To practice organizing major ideas in outline form

Levels Intermediate to advanced

Group Size Dyads

Materials A topic or sentence outline without the Roman numerals and capital letters. The outline should be typed double spaced, mounted on cardboard, and cut into segments. The pieces should then be placed into an envelope labeled with the topic of the outline. The teacher should keep a card with the completed outline in correct form, so that students can check their outline against the card.

Procedure Divide the class into pairs. Give each pair an envelope. Tell students that the pieces of the outline can be organized to form the skeleton of a composition. When the pieces have been organized in logical form, students may then record their outline on paper or on the blackboard, adding the Roman numerals, capital letters, and so on.

Example of Outline to Be Cut into Pieces

The Process of Calling Long Distance

Placing a long-distance call can be accomplished in four simple steps:

Locating the telephone number
   Calling information in local area
   Using operator assistance for overseas
Finding necessary codes
   Area codes for the United States
   Country and city codes for overseas
Placing the call
   Calling through the operator
   Dialing direct
Charges for long distance
   Lower rates on weekends and at nights

Differing rates in other countries

Summary of steps

Outline should follow this form:

Thesis:

I.   IV.
   A.   A.
   B.   B.
II.
   A.   V.
   B.
III.
   A.
   B.

EXERCISE 9: BRAINTEASERS

Affective Purposes
To share language skills to solve a puzzle
To have fun with symbols and words

Linguistic Purposes
To translate visual symbols into written communication
To develop understanding of idioms

Levels   Advanced beginning to advanced

Group Size   Groups of 3–4 members each

Materials   Brainteasers handout

Procedure
1. Tell groups that they have 10 minutes to translate the 20 brainteasers found on the handout (Figure 3.6) into a word or short phrase. Some of the phrases are American idioms.
2. Demonstrate to the class by working through one of the brainteasers with them.

BRAINTEASERS

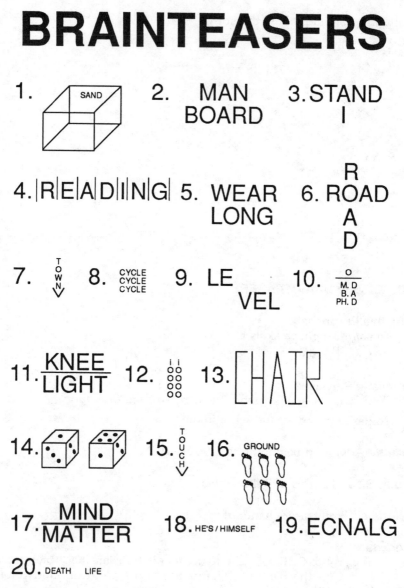

Figure 3.6   Brainteasers handout.

3. Have the group with the most right answers explain their puzzle to the class. Discuss words or phrases that individual students may not understand.

Answers

1. Sandbox	11. Neon lights
2. Man overboard	12. Circles under the eyes
3. I understand	13. High chair
4. Reading between the lines	14. Paradise
5. Long underwear	15. Touchdown
6. Crossroads	16. Six feet underground
7. Downtown	17. Mind over matter
8. Tricycle	18. He's beside himself
9. Bi-level	19. Backwards glance
10. Three degrees below zero	20. Life after death

Variation If you wish, this puzzle can be turned into a game with the highest scoring team winning a prize.

Source John W. Newstrom and James E. Scannell. *Games Trainers Play.* New York: McGraw-Hill, 1980, pp. 75 and 77. Used with permission.

EXERCISE 10: COUNT THE Ss

Affective Purposes
To illustrate that people see what they want to see

To encourage careful observation

Linguistic Purposes
To read for a specific purpose

To practice separating meaning from details

Levels Beginning to advanced

Group Size Individuals, then dyads

Materials Handout

Procedure
1. Pass out, face down, copies of the handout. When everyone has a copy, ask them to turn over their papers and to count the number of Ss, circling them as they count.

Handout:

Count the S's

THIS CLASS IS A GOOD GROUP
OF STUDENTS WHO WILL LEARN
ENGLISH AND SOON SPEAK LIKE
PEOPLE WHO WERE BORN HERE.

2. Allow about two minutes and then ask, "How many of you have the paper with 8 or 9 Ss? Who has 10 or 11 Ss on their paper?" Have students with fewer Ss marked on their papers check with a student with 11, the correct number, to see what they missed.

Variation   Follow up the exercise with a brief discussion of how we sometimes have difficulty completing a task when small details catch our attention. The exercise, plus discussion, can lead to a descriptive writing or speaking assignment in which details of person, place, or thing are important; for example, describe your favorite restaurant, a person who means a great deal to you, or an article that has special importance to you.

EXERCISE 11: FRIENDLY FRUIT

Affective Purposes
To illustrate the importance of individual characteristics
To practice observational skills

Linguistic Purposes
To practice description using color, texture, smell, etc.
To use comparison/contrast vocabulary

Levels   Beginning to advanced

Group Size   Total class

Materials   An orange (or other fruit) for each class member

Procedure
1. Give one orange to each student. Tell students to examine their oranges carefully by feeling them, smelling them, squeezing them gently, rolling them on their desks, and, in general, inspecting them carefully. Ask them to become well acquainted with their oranges, maybe even choosing names for them.
2. As soon as they have had a few minutes to inspect their oranges, collect all of the fruit and mix it up in view of the class.
3. Spread all of the oranges on a table and ask students to come forward to choose their own special orange. If arguments develop over which orange is whose, just take note of the disagreement and give one orange to each person.
4. Discuss the following questions:
   a. How many of you are sure you got your original orange? How do you know? (Allow each student to describe his or her orange briefly.)
   b. What similarities are there between telling differences between many oranges and telling differences between many people? What differences are there?
   c. Why can't we get to know people just as fast as we did our oranges? What role does the skin play—for oranges and for people?
   d. From this discussion, can you make a general statement about human actions and behavior?

Variations   (1) This exercise can be used before a descriptive writing assignment to sharpen students' sensitivity to individual differences, to concrete language, and to details. (2) The exercise can be used without the discussion questions, followed by the assignment of writing a paragraph describing each student's orange. The paragraph should begin with a main idea, or generalization, about the orange followed by individual sentences that describe the appearance, taste, texture, and smell of the orange.

EXERCISE 12: OLD OR YOUNG WOMAN?

Affective Purposes
   To illustrate the impact of people's backgrounds or attitudes on their perception of an object or event

   To open minds to new ideas and new learning

Linguistic Purposes
   To express opinions

   To practice comparison/contrast vocabulary

Levels   Intermediate to advanced

Group Size   Class divided into two groups

Materials   Old or Young Woman handout

Procedure
1. While one half of the class is doing another assignment, show the picture (Figure 3.7) to the other half, quietly telling them that it is a picture of an ugly old woman who is poorly dressed. Then ask how many of them can clearly see the old woman.
2. While the first group continues to study the picture for details, show it to the second group. Tell the second group that they will see a pretty, rich young woman who has a fancy hairdo. Ask how many of them can clearly see this young woman.
3. Address the entire class, asking students if they are able to see both the young and the old woman in the picture.

Discussion Questions
1. Why did most of the first group see an ugly old woman in the picture? And why did the second group see the young, rich woman?
2. How does what we expect to see influence what we see? (Or, for a more advanced group, how does our mental attitude influence our perception?)
3. What other expectations or attitudes do we have that influence daily activities?
4. Did you expect your English classes in the United States to be taught in the same way as English was taught in your country? How are classes different? Has this difference affected your study of English in the United States? How?
5. How can we open up our minds to new teaching methods? New learning? New ideas?

Variation   Base a writing assignment on one of the questions discussed above.

EXERCISE 13: THE FARMER'S LAND

Affective Purposes
To solve a spatial puzzle in a logical manner

To work together on a creative task

Linguistic Purposes
To practice the vocabulary of suggestions (*I think* . . ., *What if* . . ., *Let's* . . .)

To practice the conditional (*if* clauses)

Figure 3.7   Old or Young Woman handout.

Levels   Advanced beginning to advanced

Group Size   Triads

Materials   Farmer's Land handout

Procedure
1. Give each group a handout (Figure 3.8, top) illustrating the shape of a piece of land.
2. Explain the task: A farmer has died. His four sons must divide his land into four pieces of equal size and shape. Each son must have a whole piece of land; in other words, he cannot have separate pieces.
3. Allow 10–15 minutes for groups to work out a solution. Have one of the successful groups share their solution (Figure 3.8, bottom) by diagraming it on the chalkboard.

Source   Norman R. Maier. *Problem Solving and Creativity in Individuals and Groups.* Belmont, CA: Brooks/Cole, 1970, pp. 96–97. Used with permission.

EXERCISE 14: DETECTIVE STORY

Affective Purpose
To promote cooperative problem solving

Linguistic Purposes
To practice using prepositions of location such as *next to* and *to the right*

To practice using *if* clauses

To practice inferential reading

Levels   Intermediate to advanced

Group Size   Triads

Materials   Detective Story handout

Procedure
1. Tell the class that they are going to solve a murder mystery by working in groups of three students each. Give each student a handout and have them read the story.
2. After discussing any questions about vocabulary, instruct the triads to discuss the story, paying particular attention to the clues 1 through 5. Suggest that they mark names on the handout as they discover who each person is.

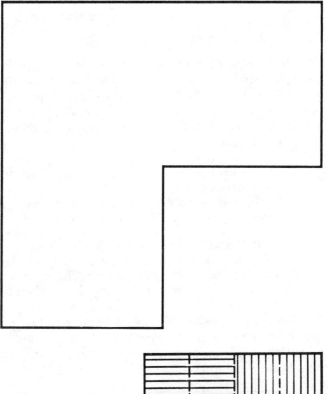

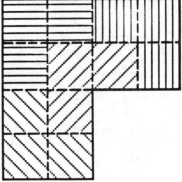

Figure 3.8   Top: Farmer's Land handout.
Bottom: Solution to the Farmer's Land.

3. If students have difficulty getting started, give them this hint: Begin
   with clue 5. We know Mr. Hill is seated in a chair which must be
   at position A since someone is seated next to him on his left. Mr.
   Hill is the dentist.
4. The group to solve the murder first should explain to the class how
   they arrived at their solution.

Detective Story Handout

Jonathan has been found dead in the library of his large home. Evidently his wine was poisoned. There are four men in the library, two sitting on a sofa and two seated in chairs near the fireplace. They are discussing the terrible murder. Their names are Mr. Hill, Mr. Smith, Mr. Jones, and Mr. Wilson. One of them is a banker, one an accountant, one a salesman, and one a dentist.

1. The servant enters and pours a whiskey for Mr. Jones and a beer for Mr. Smith.
2. In the mirror over the fireplace, the banker sees the door close behind the servant. He turns to speak to Mr. Wilson, who is next to him.
3. Neither Mr. Hill nor Mr. Smith has any sisters.
4. The accountant does not drink liquor of any kind.
5. Mr. Hill, who is sitting in one of the chairs, is the salesman's brother-in-law. The accountant is next to Mr. Hill on his left.

Suddenly a hand moves quickly to put something in Mr. Jones's whiskey. It is the murderer. No one has left his seat and no one else is in the room. What is the occupation of each man? Where is each one sitting? Who is the murderer?

Solution   Mr. Smith is the murderer. A is Mr. Hill, the dentist; B is Mr. Wilson, the accountant; C is Mr. Smith, the banker; and D is Mr. Jones, the salesman.

Source   Adapted from S. Bianchi, J. Butler, and D. Richey. *Warmups for Meeting Leaders*. San Diego: University Associates, 1990, p. 62. Used with permission.

EXERCISE 15: LEAD ME THROUGH THE MAZE

Affective Purposes
To develop trust between a leader and a follower

To experience the effects of communication in accomplishing a task

Linguistic Purposes
To practice using the vocabulary of directions

To practice imperatives (*go, watch out, turn*, etc.)

To follow directions

Levels   All levels

Group Size   Dyads

Materials   Maze handout for each participant, blindfolds for each dyad

Procedure
1. Tell the class that they are going to lead or be led through a maze on paper. Give an example on the chalkboard of what a maze is. Tell students that the key to getting out of the maze is to listen carefully to directions given by the leader. Instruct leaders to use specific language, such as *right, left, straight ahead, back*, and so on.
2. Divide the class into dyads, and instruct partners to designate one the leader and the other the follower.
3. Give a blindfold to the follower. When the follower has put on the blindfold, give a copy of the maze handout (Figure 3.9) to the leader and instruct him to place a pencil in the follower's hand and to place the point of the pencil on the entrance point of the maze.
4. Instruct dyads in the rules: no crossing of lines, directions should be given verbally with no guiding of hands by leader. If a line is crossed, the follower must move back to the space and continue.
5. Go!
6. When the follower has completed the maze, change roles and have the leader don the blindfold and, with a new Maze handout, begin

Figure 3.9   Maze handout.

from the other end and try to complete the maze with directions from the new leader.

Variations   (1) This puzzle can be made into a game by giving a time limit. The first dyad finished is the winner. (2) If space permits, form a maze with chairs. Form dyads outside the room and blindfold followers just before entering the room. Followers enter first and are directed by leaders. A scorekeeper keeps time for each dyad and deducts points for each chair touched by followers. Dyads are given a score at the end of the maze. Scores are tallied and winners announced.

EXERCISE 16: TOOTHPICKS

Affective Purposes
To discover different approaches to helping others complete a task

To develop identification with a group

Linguistic Purposes
To use spatial directions (*next to, beside, above, below,* etc.)

To use the imperative form of verbs

To follow directions

Levels   All levels

Group Size   Triads

Materials   24 toothpicks for each team

Procedure
1. Explain to students that teams of three will try to solve a puzzle using toothpicks. Two students in the team will be bosses and one student will be the worker. The workers can only follow directions given by the bosses; they cannot speak or attempt to solve the problem themselves.
2. Divide into triads and have students select roles of workers or bosses.
3. Distribute the toothpicks and direct teams to make a square similar to one drawn on poster paper or on the chalkboard.
4. When squares of toothpicks have been formed, write the statement of the problem on the chalkboard and answer any questions:

Problem: Take away eight toothpicks so that there are only two squares left.

5. Remind teams that only the bosses may speak and the worker must follow their directions and cannot attempt to solve the puzzle by him- or herself. Explain that when a team solves the puzzle, they should quietly raise their hands and not allow other teams to see their solution. Signal teams to begin.
6. If teams do not have a solution at the end of three minutes, have the worker exchange places with one of the bosses. Allow another three-minute session.
7. Call time. Ask the team that finished first to explain their solution (Figure 3.10) to the rest of the class.

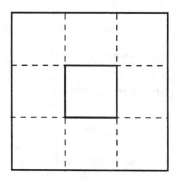

Figure 3.10 Solution to Toothpick Puzzle.

EXERCISE 17: SCHOOL SUBJECTS

Affective Purpose
To have fun solving a word puzzle

Linguistic Purposes
To use word manipulation to solve a puzzle

To use imperative forms (*put, place,* etc.)

To learn spelling of school subjects

Levels All levels

Group Size Triads

Materials Copies of the seven-piece word puzzle for each triad

Procedure
1. Form triads and distribute puzzles (Figure 3.11, top) (in envelopes) to each team.

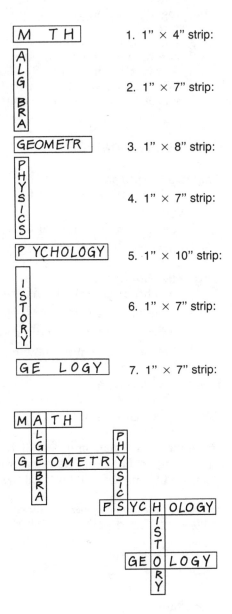

1. 1" × 4" strip:

2. 1" × 7" strip:

3. 1" × 8" strip:

4. 1" × 7" strip:

5. 1" × 10" strip:

6. 1" × 7" strip:

7. 1" × 7" strip:

Figure 3.11 Top: How to make a crossword puzzle. Bottom: Solution to crossword puzzle.

2. Explain to students that the seven words, which are all subjects in school, will fit together into a crossword puzzle. Ask them to work together, using as much spoken language as possible, to solve the puzzle.
3. Each member of the first team to finish may use the extra time before other teams complete the puzzle to learn to spell the seven words. Each member may choose three of the words to learn.
4. When all teams have finished, have the winning team spell their words for the class (see Figure 3.11, bottom).

EXERCISE 18: DOMINOES

Affective Purposes
To enhance awareness of factors that help or hinder effective communication

To discover how communication affects task-oriented behavior

To practice shared responsibility in completion of a task

Linguistic Purposes
To practice imperative forms of verbs (*put, place, position*, etc.)

To practice using *first, second, third*

To practice vocabulary of directions and positions

To practice giving and following directions

Levels   All levels

Group Size   Groups of four

Materials   Two matching sets of three dominoes each are required for each four-person team. The number of boxes of dominoes needed can be calculated from the chart that follows:

Boxes of dominoes	Maximum number of groups	Unused dominoes
2	9	2
4	18	4
6	28	0

Procedure
1. Introduce the activity by telling students that they will practice giving and following directions in groups of four. Their exercise materials will be dominoes.

2. Divide into teams of four and ask members to name themselves A, B, C, and D.
3. Direct members of each group to seat themselves, so that A and B are sitting back to back and C and D are sitting where they can watch A and B. Announce that A and B will work on a task while C and D observe them.
4. Give A and B from each group one of the matched sets of three dominoes, which they may compare. Also give each one a lapboard on which to work.
5. A is instructed to make a design with dominoes on the lapboard. Once it is made, it is not to be changed.
6. C and D are to observe A and B, paying special attention to what kind of language helps communication. They are not to talk to A or B.
7. A instructs B on how to make a design identical to his or her own. A and B may talk freely as B attempts to duplicate A's design.
8. After A has given what seems to be adequate instructions to B, the pair may turn around and compare designs.
9. C and D give brief feedback on instructions that seemed most helpful.
10. All participants rotate places, repeating the activity until each has had a turn giving directions.
11. Debrief the activity with a short discussion of the words and phrases that helped or hindered communication.

Variations   Tinkertoys or blocks may be used instead of dominoes.

EXERCISE 19: THE DETECTIVE

Affective Purposes
   To explore the relationship among observation, knowledge, and inference

   To increase awareness of how prejudices and assumptions influence our perceptions

Linguistic Purposes
   To practice making inferences from reading and observation

   To relate our own experiences to what we read and observe

Levels   Intermediate to advanced

Group Size   Total class for first half of activity; groups of 4–5 members each for second half of exercise

Materials   Each participant should have the following: a Detective room description sheet, a Detective room diagram, a Detective inference sheet, newsprint, and a felt-tip marker for each group

Procedure
1. Introduce the activity by saying: "Today we're going to play detective. As you know, detectives like Sherlock Holmes pay careful attention to the process of connecting three things: (a) observation, (b) knowledge, and (c) induction and deduction (inference)." Have students give their interpretations of the three terms, and then add further information: "By observation, we mean what you see; by knowledge, what meanings, information, and facts you have available to draw upon; by deduction, that mental process by which you reason from the general to the specific (all human beings breathe; this child is a human being; therefore, this child breathes); and by induction, the mental process of reasoning from the specific to the general (every high school I have ever seen teaches mathematics; therefore, all high schools teach mathematics).
2. Give each student a Detective room description sheet and a Detective room diagram. Tell students to read the room description and study the diagram carefully.
3. After students have had time to complete the activity above, have them form groups of four to discuss their observations and inferences and to fill out the inference sheets.
4. Reassemble the entire group and initiate a discussion in one or more of the following ways:
   a. Select individual students to summarize their profiles for the group.
   b. Call on each student to give a major observation and inference while you list them on newsprint or the chalkboard.
   c. Have each student give a one-word or one-sentence description of the president. List these on newsprint or on the chalkboard.

Detective Room Description Sheet

   The president of the ALTA Communications company disappeared from the executive office two days ago. Neither the family nor business associates have heard from the president. You have just arrived at the

ALTA Company to investigate the executive office. As you pass through the heavy carved wooden door, you are very curious about the person who has disappeared.

A faint smell of perfume or incense leads you into the room. You notice that the soft rose-colored carpeting is so thick that your steps cannot be heard. To the left of the doorway are two beige armchairs and a tall Southwestern style lamp with a shade of muted rose, lavender, and beige. Between the chairs is a low table with a large glass ashtray, filled with two cigarette butts, one marked with bright red lipstick. Next to the ashtray is a book of matches marked "New Orleans Jazz Club."

You sit in one of the chairs and observe the rest of the office. A large picture window with lightweight beige and rose striped drapes is to your left. In front of the window is a sofa, also striped in beige and rose, with several rose pillows tossed on it. Next to the sofa is a small table with an open briefcase. You get up from your chair to inspect the briefcase. It is filled with file folders marked *Urgent* in addition to unopened business letters. In fact, it is so full that you cannot close it.

You replace the briefcase and sit on the sofa. To your left is a huge walnut desk. On top of the polished desk is a silver-framed photograph of two boys, about eight and ten years old, and a small black dog. Also on the desk are a beige telephone, a date book lying open on top of a Snickers candy bar, a pile of open file folders, a few sheets of blank paper, and a gold pen and pencil set. Behind the desk is a computer on a computer table. The computer is still on. Unopened mail is scattered next to the computer keyboard.

Behind the desk are floor to ceiling shelves with sets of encyclopedias, business books, and a collection of sports trophies. The trophies are for basketball and soccer championships. There is also a small bowling trophy sitting next to an antique clock. An empty wastebasket sits next to the desk. You rise from the chair and inspect the contents of the wastebasket. In it you find a discarded chocolate bar wrapper, two ticket stubs from a White Sox ball game, and a Kleenex with the same red lipstick on it. Next to the wastebasket is a small stack of magazines, including *Time*, *Sports Illustrated*, *Psychology Today*, *New Woman*, and *Business World*.

As you replace the contents of the wastebasket, you notice a newspaper under the desk. It is open to the travel section. An ad, "Escape to the Tahitian Islands," is circled in red. The telephone rings and you stop to answer it. . . .

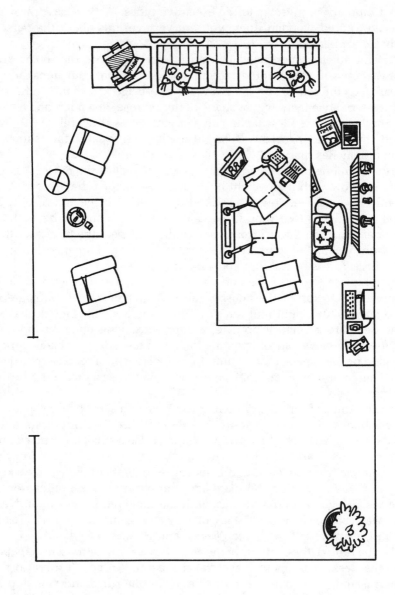

Detective Inference Sheet

Read the Detective room description sheet and study the diagram carefully. Then complete the Detective inference sheet as follows:

1. In the left-hand column (Observation), write down data from your reading that you think are important clues about what kind of person the president is and what has happened to the president.
2. In the middle column (Knowledge), note any experiences that you may have had that influence your observation.
3. In the right-hand column (Inference), write whatever conclusions you have reached as a result of your observations.

Observation	Knowledge	Inference

4

Competitive Games

Games have five basic characteristics, according to T. S. Rodgers: they are competitive, governed by rules, goal-defined, engaging in that they challenge the participants, and, last, they have closure or a predetermined point at which they are finished.[1]

Games can create a sense of fun and healthy competition that stimulates natural and purposeful use of language. Games can be used as dynamic warm-ups, for team building, or simply to wake up a sleepy group and give them energy for the rest of the class period.

EXERCISE 1: FAMOUS PEOPLE

Affective Purpose
To promote interaction among all members of the class

Linguistic Purposes
To practice question/answer format (*Are you . . .? Yes, I am/No, I'm not; Were you . . .?*, etc.)

To use vocabulary related to historical and popular persons

Levels   Beginning to advanced

Group Size   Total group

Materials   Paper and pins

Procedure
1. As each student enters the classroom, pin the name of a famous person or character on his or her back. The name should be internationally recognized, not bound to U.S. culture, such as Albert Schweitzer, John F. Kennedy, Martin Luther King, Mickey Mouse, Snoopy, Garfield, Queen Elizabeth, Confucius, Marie Curie, or Plato.
2. Students are instructed to guess the name of the person on their back by asking one question of each student. Questions can be

answered by either a "yes" or "no" followed by the appropriate phrase. (For example: "Is this person still alive?" "Yes, he is.") After the student receives an answer, he or she should move on and ask another student the next question.
3. The first person to guess his or her identity is the winner. After the winner has been announced, allow five more minutes for students to try to find out their identities.

EXERCISE 2: MEMORY QUIZ

Affective Purposes
To use short-term memory

To have fun with a simple game

Linguistic Purposes
To stimulate recall of items in the target language

To increase vocabulary

Levels   Beginning to advanced

Group Size   Total group

Materials   Tray of small items

Procedure
1. Before class, prepare a tray with 20 items that suit the level of English of the group and your purpose for the exercise. (For example, if the group has been studying vocabulary of food, you might include food items on the tray. If you just want to stimulate recall of general vocabulary, include items that are unrelated.) Cover the tray with a cloth.
2. Tell students that they will have one minute to look at the objects on the tray. They will then be asked to write down as many things as they can remember.
3. Move around the classroom, giving small groups of students one minute to observe the objects on the tray. Cover the tray as you move to the next group.
4. After all students have had a chance to see the objects, cover the tray and instruct them to write down as many items as they can remember. Ask for volunteers to read their lists. The winner is the student who has the most correct items written down.

EXERCISE 3: COMPETITION BEE

Affective Purposes
To liven up a low-energy group
To experience a friendly spirit of competition

Linguistic Purpose
To practice grammar points, vocabulary, spelling, or other subjects of current study

Levels Beginning to advanced

Group Size Total group

Materials Teacher's list of questions

Procedure This game is very much like the old-fashioned spelling bee. A competition bee can be used as a warm-up exercise or as a way of reinforcing vocabulary, spelling words, grammar points, or other information of interest to the group, such as world capitals.

1. Form a circle of chairs, but ask participants to stand up in front of their chairs.
2. Go around the group, quickly asking questions from a list of 50 or 60. For example, if your topic for the bee is past tense, ask for the past tense of present tense verbs. For example, "Abdulla, fight." Abdulla responds, "Fought." "Lee, write." "Wrote," Lee answers.
3. If a student misses, he or she is asked to sit down until the next game. The last person standing wins the bee.

EXERCISE 4: SCAVENGER HUNT

Affective Purposes
To get students to speak to persons they may not know
To immerse students in a task-oriented activity

Linguistic Purposes
To practice introductions
To practice question/answer format
To practice expressions of gratitude

Levels   Beginning to advanced

Group Size   Teams of 4-6 students each

Materials   Lists of items to obtain

Procedure
1. After dividing the group into teams, give the teams a specific time period for completing their task and certain boundaries within which they will work (for example, within the school building or on Main Street from the drugstore to the antique shop). Instruct students to take turns asking for objects or information.
2. Then provide each team with the same list of objects to obtain. In order to promote language use, include items that must be asked for, not ones that are openly available.

Examples of lists:

College Scavenger Hunt

Find the following items or information:

1. A map of the library
2. A #67 bus schedule
3. An overseas postage stamp
4. The hours for open swimming
5. A college schedule of classes for next semester
6. Information about financial aid for international students
7. A list of exhibits scheduled for the art museum next month
8. Information about who won the intramural volleyball competition
9. Information about when the play tryouts are scheduled
10. A list of new books in the library

Main Street Scavenger Hunt

1. Visit the post office to buy a postcard.
2. Visit the Old Shoppe to find out how old the oldest antique in the shop is.
3. Visit the pharmacy to find out if you can buy penicillin without a prescription.

4. Visit the card shop to ask if they have greeting cards in other languages.
5. Visit the deli in the supermarket to ask if they have Greek salad.
6. Get a free sample of chocolate candy from the Sweet Shop.
7. Visit the Oriental Emporium to get the owner's business card.
8. Visit the meat department of Safeway to get a package of free dog bones.
9. Visit the Texaco station to get a free state road map.
10. Visit the Shoe Shop to ask how much it costs to have new rubber heels put on your shoes.

EXERCISE 5: COMPETING FOR "CASH"

Affective Purposes
To use competition and rewards to stimulate learning

To have fun

Linguistic Purpose
To practice any grammar or vocabulary items currently being studied

Levels Beginning to advanced

Group Size Two teams of two persons each, remainder of class

Materials Flip charts, newsprint pages, or two large display boards; play money; handouts of questions listed on charts.

Procedure
1. Select a set of items that students are to have learned, such as five sentences some of which have subject-verb agreement errors or a set of prefixes, affixes, and suffixes with their meanings, some of which are incorrect.
2. Print these items on the flip chart pages or attach them to the two large display boards. Place the charts or boards so class members cannot see them.
3. Next choose teams of two persons each to work at each chart or board. Their objective is to place an X next to each of the correct items before the end of a specified time limit.
4. Students who are not on the teams are assigned the same task at their desks. When the time limit is up, the teacher stops the action.
5. The boards or charts are then turned toward the class and students are asked to spot errors in the other team's responses. Students identifying an error and correcting it are given a play dollar.
6. The teacher then determines which team has the most correct responses and awards the team a five dollar "bill."

7. The game continues with two new teams tackling another set of items.

EXERCISE 6: DO AS I SAY

Affective Purpose
To help students see tasks through the eyes of another person

Linguistic Purposes
To practice giving specific directions

To practice imperative forms of verbs (*put, join, connect,* etc.)

To practice speaking in the second person (*you*)

To practice questions beginning with *should, where, how,* etc.

Levels   Intermediate to advanced

Group Size   Dyads

Materials   A large set of Legos or Tinkertoys, copies for one student in each dyad of a diagram of a simple model of something to construct. (Diagrams can be obtained with boxes of Legos or Tinkertoys.)

Procedure
1. Provide each pair with an adequate number of Legos or Tinkertoys to make the model depicted on the handout.
2. Have each pair decide who will give instructions and who will build the model. Tell students that the model builder may ask questions if necessary. The student giving instructions must not show the handout to the builder nor can he or she help the builder by touching the building materials.
3. Signal students to begin the task. The first pair to complete the task before the time allotted is the winner. If no pair completes the task, the winner is the pair which has the most completed.

EXERCISE 7: WHO AM I?

Affective Purposes
To encourage using the imagination

To work together as a group toward a solution

Linguistic Purposes
To practice questions and statements in the first and third person

To practice formulating appropriate questions and answers that help team members reach a solution

Levels Beginning to advanced

Group Size Two teams

Materials Cards with names of famous persons

Procedure
1. Each team chooses a leader, who will answer questions from team members. Set a time limit within which the team must come up with an answer.
2. The first team chooses a card from a stack turned facedown. On the card is the name of a famous person. Team members ask the leader questions, that can be answered by "Yes, I am," "No I'm not," or "I don't know." For example, the leader might choose a card with the name "Marie Curie" printed on it. A student on the team says, "Are you American?" The leader responds, "No, I'm not." The team member then asks, "Are you from Europe?" "Yes, I am," the leader says. Another team member asks, "Are you living?" "No, I'm not," the leader answers. The questions and answers continue.
3. If the team guesses the famous person within the time limit, it gets one point, and the other team draws a card and tries to guess. If the team does not guess correctly within the time allotted, the other team is given an opportunity to get the correct answer within the same time frame.
4. The team which has the highest number of correct guesses is the winner.

Sample list of famous persons Marie Curie, Abraham Lincoln, Christopher Columbus, Albert Schweitzer, Moses, Isaac Newton, Albert Einstein, George Washington, Jacqueline Kennedy, Marilyn Monroe, Martin Luther King, Tom Selleck, Anwar Sadat, Omar Sharif, Karl Marx, Ronald Reagan, John F. Kennedy.

Variations Use characters from stories or a novel that students have read as a class assignment. For lower-level students, change the game to What Am I? and work with common objects in the classroom or in a room of the house, food items, or whatever students have been working on to develop their vocabulary.

EXERCISE 8: DOUBLE OR QUITS

Affective Purposes
To develop a spirit of team cooperation
To have fun competing with another team

Linguistic Purposes
To develop a critical "ear" for mistakes in grammar
To practice grammar points studied in class

Levels   Beginning to advanced

Group Size   Dyads

Materials   Sentences including grammar points studied in class, some sentences correct and others with errors; coins or play money

Procedure
1. Explain to the dyads that they are going to compete in an oral grammar quiz. The aim of each pair is to win as much money as possible.
2. Tell the first pair that you are going to read a sentence that they will judge to be correct or incorrect. Then read the first sentence from the quiz sheet. (Remember that incorrect sentences should be read convincingly, so students cannot tell by the tone of your voice that something is wrong with the sentence.)
3. Ask, "Correct or incorrect?" Give the team time for a quick consultation (no more than 20 seconds on a timer). If they answer "Correct" and the sentence is correct, give them two coins. If they answer "Incorrect" and they are right, reply, "Please correct the sentence." If they make an accurate correction, give them five coins.
4. Now offer them the chance of "double or quits." If they choose to double, read them another sentence. If they answer incorrectly, they lose the money they have already won. If they answer correctly, they win the same prize money as they won on the first sentence. If they choose to quit, move on and offer the second sentence to the second pair. Do not offer "double or quits" when a team has successfully answered their second question—turn to another team.

Try to work through the sentences at a fast pace, enforcing the 20-second rule by having a watch or timer in front of you.

EXERCISE 9: BARGAINING FOR RESOURCES

Affective Purposes
To experience the process of bargaining

To observe what happens when there is an uneven distribution of necessities

Linguistic Purposes
To practice conversing in a variety of tenses

To afford practice in speaking spontaneously

Levels Intermediate to advanced

Group Size Four groups of 3–5 students each

Materials A Bargaining for Resources tasks sheet for each group, four envelopes containing materials as follows:

Group 1:   Scissors, ruler, paper clips, pencils, two 4" squares of red paper and two of white

Group 2:   Scissors, glue and 8½" × 11" sheets of paper (two blue, two white, two gold)

Group 3:   Felt-tip markers and 8½" × 11" sheets of paper (two green, two white, two gold)

Group 4:   8½" × 11" sheets of paper (one each of green, gold, red, and purple)

Physical Setting Table and chairs for each group, or student desks placed in a circle, far enough away from each other so that one group cannot hear strategies planned by another group.

Procedure
1. When groups are seated at their individual tables, distribute an envelope of materials and a tasks sheet to each group.
2. Ask the group not to open their materials until you tell them to begin the task. Then explain that each group has different materials but that each group must complete the same tasks. Explain that they may bargain with any other group for the use of materials and tools in any way the groups agree on. Emphasize that the first group to complete all tasks is the winner.

3. Tell groups that when you tell them to begin they should read their tasks and look over their resources to see what is needed to complete their tasks and what resources they can use to bargain with. For example, one group might trade a pair of scissors for a felt-tip marker. Then they should choose a leader to go out to other groups to search for needed resources and to bargain for them. They may change leaders during the process if they wish to.
4. Give the signal to begin and observe the groups so that you can supply feedback during debriefing. Note which group finishes first, second, and so on. Stop the process when all groups have finished their tasks.

Debriefing
1. Which group had the most resources?
2. Which had the fewest resources?
3. How did you feel when you found out what you needed from other groups?
4. How did you choose your leader? Did you change leaders? Why or why not?
5. Did your group exchange one resource for another? Did you share resources?
6. What made the winning group finish their task first?
7. Can you compare this activity to relationships among nations in the world today?
8. How do the more powerful groups relate to the less powerful ones?

Bargaining for Resources Tasks Sheet

Each group is to complete the following tasks:

1. Make a 3" × 3" square of white paper.
2. Make a 4" × 2" rectangle of gold paper.
3. Make a four-link paper chain, each link of a different color.
4. Make a T-shaped piece 3" × 5" with green and white paper.

The first group to complete all tasks is the winner. Groups may bargain with other groups for the use of materials and tools to complete the tasks.

EXERCISE 10: YOU TEST US AND WE'LL TEST YOU

Affective Purpose
To develop a spirit of cooperation centered around a task.

Linguistic Purposes
To review grammar points, reading comprehension, or vocabulary being used in a particular class

To practice writing clear specific questions

Levels Beginning to advanced

Group Size Groups of 2–4 students each

Materials 3″ × 5″ lined note cards for questions

Procedure
1. Divide the class into an even number of groups (2–4 students each). Give each group a number designation and tell them to sit apart from the other groups.
2. Explain that each group will make up a test for another group. The test will include 10 questions about _____ (the story they have just read, present perfect tense, passive voice, vocabulary, etc.). The questions will be in the form of _____ (multiple choice, fill in the blank, short answer, etc.). Have examples of the types of questions from which they may choose on the chalkboard or posted around the room.
3. The finished test of 10 questions will be given to the other team. Team members may discuss all questions before choosing answers. Ten points will be given for each correct answer.
4. Announce that each group should begin by discussing what items they would like to include on the test. Allow about 10 minutes for discussion and assignment of question areas to specific team members. Allow another 10–15 minutes for team members to write questions and record each one on a note card. Circulate among groups to answer any questions about procedure or about test items.
5. When questions are completed, ask someone in the group to read them aloud in order to check clarity and correctness. Also have the group provide answers. (Do not write the answers on the cards.)
6. Groups exchange cards and answer the set of questions by recording answers on a separate note card. Cards can be distributed individually to students for their consideration of questions and then discussed as a group with a recorder marking answers on a note card. Ten minutes can be allowed for answers.

7. Return test cards and answer card to the group which formulated the questions. This group checks answers and gives a total score (10 points each) for number correct. Answer card is returned to group.
8. If any revision of questions is needed, give time for rewriting.
9. Process can be repeated with different test cards circulated to groups.

EXERCISE 11: X IN THE SQUARE

Affective Purposes
To enjoy a spirit of fun while learning

To demonstrate how cooperation and competition can affect winning and losing

Linguistic Purposes
To discuss solutions to a problem

To practice modals (*can, could, might, must, ought to,* etc.)

Levels Beginning to advanced

Group Size Groups of 2–8 students each

Materials One felt-tip marker of a different color for each team; one sheet of newsprint, with the chart of 36 squares drawn on it, for each pair of teams

Procedure
1. Display a chart of squares (Figure 4.1) for students to see. Explain that this game will be carried out by two teams, using the chart and felt-tip markers. Each team will use a different-colored marker to place an X in a square during the group's turn. The object is to complete rows (horizontal, vertical, or diagonal) of five squares marked with Xs of the group's color. (Demonstrate horizontal, etc., by marking the demonstration sheet.) A team will mark only one X in a square each turn; then the other team will do the same. Teams are allowed just 30 seconds for each turn. However, each team will be given 10 minutes before the first turn to discuss their plan for winning. The game will be finished when each group has had the chance to take 15 turns.
2. Tell teams who their competition is and instruct each team to meet for 10 minutes to plan its strategy and to choose a "marker" who will draw the Xs in the team's chosen squares on the newsprint. The "marker" can talk to his or her group before each turn but must stay within the 30-second time limit per turn.

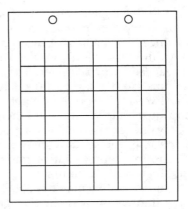

Figure 4.1 Chart of squares.

3. Flip a coin to decide which team goes first. Teams then move alternately until each group has had a chance to move 15 times. Keep the groups within the 30-second time limit for each turn.

Variations Each team can be given 20 letters (consonants and vowels) to use in building words by entering a letter in a square. Points can be given for the number of words completed by each team or for the number of letters used by each team.

EXERCISE 12: RIDDLES

Affective Purposes
To cooperate in solving riddles

To experience dependence on others for completion of a task

Linguistic Purposes
To practice questions, such as *Do you have . . .?* and *May I have . . .?*

To practice language of negotiations, such as *I'll give you this piece for that one* or *If you give me that one, I'll give you this one.*

Levels Intermediate to advanced

Group Size Four groups of 2–5 students each

Materials Four envelopes with 3″ × 5″ cards typed with a line of a riddle (see directions for making riddles envelope sets)

Procedure

1. After forming four groups, give each a letter: A, B, C, or D. Seat the groups in separate parts of the room.
2. Announce that the task of each group will be to solve a riddle. Explain that a riddle is a word puzzle. For example, what is black and white and read all over? (Answer: The newspaper.) To win the game, each team must do two things: (a) get all the pieces of the riddle and (b) find the answer to the riddle. To get all the clues or pieces for a riddle, a group must trade or bargain for them. Rules for exchanging clues include:
   a. Only one representative of a group may leave the group at any time.
   b. Only one representative may bargain with another group at one time.
   c. A group's representative must change after each transaction with another group is completed.
   d. A representative may not obtain or give more than two clues during any transaction with another group.
3. Tell the groups to begin by reading the clues in the envelope and sorting out the clues that go with their group's letter: A, B, C, and D. After this has been accomplished, they should choose the first representative to visit another group to bargain for clues.
4. While students are working, you may circulate and tell groups when they have all the necessary pieces to solve their riddles. As soon as a group has collected all pieces and has solved its riddle, announce that group as winner but encourage other groups to work for five more minutes to see if they can solve their riddles.

Directions for Making Riddles Envelope Set

Each line of each riddle (including the letter and number) is typed on a separate 3" × 5" card. The letter must be included on the card. All cards labeled A are placed in an envelope marked "A," all Bs are placed in an envelope marked "B," and so on.

Riddle 1

A   Two workmen were repairing a roof.

D   They fell through a large chimney and landed in a fireplace on the floor below.

C   Both men were unhurt.

D   They looked at each other, walked around the room, stretched their arms, and decided they were OK.

D   Without speaking a word or talking about their accident, both men started back to their job.

C   One man's face was all black from the soot in the chimney.

D   However, the other man's face was very clean.

A   The man with the clean face went in and washed his face; however, the man with the dirty face went back to work without washing his face.

B   Can you explain why they did this?[2]

Riddle 2

A   When Jim went to buy a barrel of apple juice from Farmer Brown, the farmer had only about one-half barrel left.

B   Jim looked into the barrel and thought it was less than one-half full, while the farmer thought it was more than one-half full.

C   They talked about it and quickly decided how they would tell which one of them was right. They did not use any measuring device and they did not put anything into the barrel.

A   How did they do it?[2]

Riddle 3

B   A man lived on the twelfth floor of an apartment building.

C   Each day, when he came home from work, he took the elevator to the eighth floor, got out, and walked up to his apartment on the twelfth floor.

A   The elevator was in good operating order and went all the way to the twelfth floor.

D   Why did the man walk up those four flights of stairs?[2]

Riddle 4

B   A man has a fox, a goose, and some corn.

B   He wants to take them across a river, but he only has a tiny boat and can take only one of the three at a time.

A   If he leaves the fox with the goose, the fox will eat the goose.

C   If he leaves the goose with the corn, the goose will have a good dinner.

D   How does he get all three across the river? (Hint: The fox will not eat the corn.)

Answers to the Riddles   *Riddle 1:* Each man thought his face looked like the other's. *Riddle 2:* They tipped the barrel on the diagonal. If the liquid reached the rim and still covered the bottom, it was more than half full; if the bottom of the barrel showed, it was less than half full. *Riddle 3:* He was a midget and could not reach any button above "8" on the elevator panel. *Riddle 4:* The man takes the goose over first. He returns and takes the fox and then brings the goose back with him. He leaves it and crosses the river with the corn. Finally he returns with the goose.

EXERCISE 13: TWENTY QUESTIONS

Affective Purposes
To encourage using the imagination

To work together as a group toward a solution

Linguistic Purposes
To practice asking questions and making statements in the first and third person

To practice formulating appropriate questions and answers that help team members reach a solution

Levels   Beginning to advanced

Group Size   Two teams of any number

Materials   A set of cards marked with well-known persons, places, and things

Procedure
1. Explain that the object of Twenty Questions is to correctly identify well-known people, places, and things by asking questions. Two teams will compete against each other. For example, a team member draws the top card, which says "I am a tomato." He tells his team, "I am a thing." Team members take turns asking questions, such as, "Are you in this room?" or "Are you something to eat?" The member holding the card answers each question by saying, "Yes, I am" or "No, I'm not."
2. The rules are as follows: Only 20 questions are allowed each team. If the first team does not get the answer, the second team can guess. If a team guesses the correct person, place, or thing before using up their 20 questions, they have a second turn with a new word. Each correct answer gives a team one point. The team with the most points wins the game.
3. Choose which team goes first by tossing a coin or rolling a die.
4. Begin play with the chosen team drawing a card. Keep score on the chalkboard with Team A and Team B listed.

Twenty Questions Cards   Suggestions for persons, places, and things include Mickey Mouse, Santa Claus, Abraham Lincoln, George Washington, Adam, the teacher, Paris, New York, the Grand Canyon, the Sahara desert, a shopping center, the Atlantic Ocean, a candle, coffee, music, gold, fire, a mustache, a drum, an onion, fireworks, teeth, or the like.

Variation   Teams can make cards for each other. The teacher should review these before play begins to determine if suggested persons, places, and things are appropriate for the game.

EXERCISE 14: RUMORS

Affective Purpose
To illustrate distortions that sometimes occur when information is transmitted through several sources

Linguistic Purposes
To practice repeating correctly what one has read or heard

To use the past tense

To use reported speech

Levels   Beginning to advanced

Group Size   Two teams of 6–8 members each

Materials   Two copies of the accident report, newsprint, felt-tip marker or chalkboard and chalk, accident report written on newsprint

Procedure
1. Explain the meaning of Rumors, the title of the game (gossip; information of which the truth and source are unknown). Tell students that they will experience listening to a report of an accident, which they will then have to repeat to another person on their team. The last person on each team will be the detective who is investigating the accident. He will hear the final report and write down on newsprint what he has heard.
2. Divide the class into two teams, designating which person is the detective.
3. Arrange the teams on separate sides of the room with all but two team members waiting in one corner while the reporter and the person hearing the report are seated in chairs away from the group.
4. Give an accident report to the first member of each team and instruct them to go to the chairs designated for that team and sit down. The first member will read the accident report to the second member. The second person may only listen; he or she may not take notes. At this point, the reader returns to the group but is cautioned not to share what he has read. The third group member goes to the chairs, sits down, and listens to the report of the second person.

5. This process is repeated until all team members but the last one have had the message transmitted to them. The last person is the detective, who has the report repeated to him or her. When both teams have finished, the detectives write their reports, so the total group can read them.

6. The teacher then reveals the original accident report written on newsprint. Students compare both detectives' reports and decide which is closest to the original. The team with the Detective Report that is closest to the original written report will be the winner.

Sample Accident Report for Intermediate Level

On December 23, at 10:30 p.m., a red Ford truck was heading north on Highway 70, at approximately 60 miles per hour. When the truck reached slow-moving traffic, the driver braked and skidded on the icy road. The truck slid into the rear of a brown Toyota. The Toyota was totally wrecked and the driver, a 19-year-old woman, was killed. The driver of the truck, a 25-year-old man, suffered a broken leg and back injuries.

EXERCISE 15: PINS AND STRAWS

Affective Purposes
To develop a spirit of friendly competition between groups

To use organizational skills to complete a task

To practice cooperation

Linguistic Purposes
To practice the vocabulary of suggestions and opinions

To practice conversation related to a task

To practice the imperative form of verbs

Levels   Beginning to advanced

Group Size   Groups of 4–5 persons each.

Materials   One package of drinking straws (100 per package) for each group, one package of straight pins for each group

Procedure
1. Explain that teams will build structures made of pins and straws. Teams will discuss their project before beginning and then be given 20 minutes for the building process. At the end of 20 minutes, structures will be displayed for everyone to see. A judge from each team and the teacher will vote on which structure is the best in terms of height, strength, and beauty. Votes will be tallied for the winning structure.
2. Divide into teams and distribute pins and straws to each team.
3. Announce that there will be five minutes for a discussion of what kind of structure each team will build and how they will build it. Allow team members to use paper and pencil to sketch a design, if they wish.
4. Tell teams to begin. Give warnings at 10 and 15 minutes. Tell teams to stop when 20 minutes is up.
5. Give students a chance to circulate and look at other teams' structures.
6. Have each team choose a judge. The teacher joins the judges to rank the structures on height, strength, and beauty. The following tally sheet may be used (rank characteristics on a scale from 1 to 5, with 5 being the best).

VOTING TALLY

Team	Height	Strength	Beauty	Total
1				
2				
3				

NOTES

1. "A Framework for Making and Using Language Teaching Games." *Guidelines for Language Games*. Singapore: RELC, 1981, pp. 1–7.
2. "Riddles: Intergroup Competition," *Structured Experience Kit*. San Diego; University Associates, 1980, GTB-WIL-5-ii.

Critical Incidents and Role Plays

The two types of activities that are the focus of this chapter are closely related in that real-life situations are the material of both.

Critical incidents are descriptions of difficult or awkward situations in which cultural norms or values cause communication to break down between members of different cultures. The situations are read and discussed by members of a small group with the purpose of determining what caused the problem and what solution there might be. The use of critical incidents originated with Peace Corps training, where they were used to sensitize Peace Corps volunteers to their target cultures.

Role plays, on the other hand, do not necessarily involve a cultural misunderstanding. They are based on any real-life situation. Participants are given a skeleton description of the part they are to play and then put themselves "in the shoes" of the given person in the specific situation described; in other words, they become actors. All of the critical incidents also can be adapted to role-playing.

Students respond well to exercises based on critical incidents or on role plays because the learning process involves active participation and addresses situations that they have faced themselves or may experience in the future.

CRITICAL INCIDENTS

All of the situations used in the critical incident exercises are true experiences of international students, ESL teachers, or business people. (Cultural notes explaining individual incidents begin on p. 107.)

EXERCISE 1: HELP! I'M JUST A FOREIGN STUDENT!

Affective Purposes

To become sensitive to cultural differences regarding legal matters and the problems that can result from them

To develop solutions for cultural misunderstandings

Linguistic Purposes
To practice reading for understanding

To practice techniques of small-group discussion: listening for understanding, expressing views clearly, taking turns

Levels   High beginning to advanced

Group Size   Groups of 3–4 students each

Materials   Critical Incidents handout for each student

Procedure   Explain the meaning of critical incidents. You might say, "Critical incidents are times when something goes wrong with communication between people of different cultures. In other words, a problem is caused by not understanding each other's culture."

Tell students that after they break up into their groups, one student in each group can volunteer to read aloud the critical incident while the rest of the group follows. Then the group will discuss the questions printed at the bottom of the handout.

After each group has had time to discuss the three incidents, the instructor may wish to have each group report on its discussion of one of the incidents.

Variations   Before discussing the questions on the handout, students in each group can read the incident and then complete the Reaction Scale that follows.

Reaction Scale

Instructions   Read each incident carefully. Decide how much you agree or disagree with the actions or feelings of the international student. Select a number from the 8-point scale to indicate your reaction, and circle the number. Briefly note why you answered this way. Then indicate what you would do in this same situation. Complete the second part of the scale in the same way for the American involved in the incident.

International Student

Completely disagree		Disagree more than agree		Agree more than disagree		Completely agree	
1	2	3	4	5	6	7	8

Why?

What would you do?

American

Completely disagree		Disagree more than agree		Agree more than disagree		Completely agree	
1	2	3	4	5	6	7	8

Why?

What would you do?

Critical Incidents Handout

Instructions   Read each incident carefully and then discuss the following questions:

1. What problem has been created for the international student?
2. What problem has been created for the American?
3. What cultural misunderstanding caused the problem?
4. How would you solve the problem if you were the student?
5. Is there something you might do to ease the problem if you were the American?

A. When Khalid, a new student in the English language center, had borrowed a friend's new car to practice for the driving exam, he didn't notice that the *temporary* license plate had *expired*. As he headed toward Broadway, he *glanced* in the rearview mirror and saw the flashing lights of a police car behind him. Khalid pulled over to the curb, worried because he didn't understand what he had done.

When the officer asked him for his license, Khalid gave him the international license he had brought with him.

"What's this?" the officer asked, turning the paper over in his hand.

"License, international license," Khalid said.

"Do you have a state license?" There was a long pause before Khalid answered.

"Yes, sir."

"Well, let me see it, please."

"Next week I get license."

After trying to communicate a few more times, the officer asked for the registration and proof of insurance, which Khalid could not find. The officer gave Khalid a ticket for driving without a *valid* license and a *current* license plate and also cited him for not having proof of insurance.

temporary—for a short period of time	valid—legal
expired—no longer good	current—up-to-date
glanced—looked quickly	

B. Yasir, a community college student, went to the local supermarket to shop for groceries. After he had gone through the checkout stand with all the items he needed for the party he was having that night, he remembered that he had left some film to be printed. He picked up the film from the clerk at the Photo Counter, turned around, and met Khalifa, a friend of his from school. He and Khalifa talked for awhile about the party, and then Yasir walked out the door of the supermarket toward his car.

"Come back here, you!" a voice yelled at Yasir.

"Yes?" Yasir replied, turning to look behind him.

The assistant manager of the market took Yasir by the shoulder and led him back into the store, where he called the police. Yasir was afraid of what might happen. "Here's the money for the photos," he offered the manager, who pushed away the money. The police arrived, questioned Yasir, and gave him a paper with a date when he had to appear in court on shoplifting charges.

C. One afternoon last semester an American girl was hurrying down the hall to her physics class. She was by herself in the hall until she turned the corner by the drinking fountain where she met a group of international students who were speaking loudly in their own language.

One of the students looked at her and said something in his own language. Then he laughed. His tone of voice and his laugh made her feel very uncomfortable and quite angry. She gave the group a *dirty* look and hurried into the classroom where she met her boyfriend. She explained the incident to him.

"I felt that I was being *sexually harrassed* even though I didn't understand the words he said to me," she explained to her boyfriend. He was even angrier than she was.

"Show me who the guys are, and I'll make them *eat their words*," he said.

"No, I think it would be better to talk to the campus police," she suggested.

dirty—angry

sexual harrassment—actions or words of a sexual nature that bother someone

to eat one's words—to take back what one has said, to apologize

---

EXERCISE 2: MAY I TAKE THE TEST AGAIN?

Affective Purposes

To become aware of differences in educational systems

To become aware of the protocol of student-teacher relations in the United States

Linguistic Purposes

To use the vocabulary related to expressing opinions

To practice rules of small-group discussion

Levels   Intermediate to advanced

Group Size   Groups of 3–4 students each

Materials   Critical Incidents handout for each student

Procedure   Follow the same procedure explained in Exercise 1.

Critical Incidents Handout

Instructions   After carefully reading each critical incident, discuss the following questions:

1. What problem has been created for the international student?
2. What problem has been created for the American?
3. What cultural misunderstanding caused the problem?
4. How would you solve the problem if you were the student?
5. Is there something you might do to ease the problem if you were the American?

A. Wei Ping thought she had done very well on yesterday's history test. When the test was returned, she was surprised to find she had received only 40 percent. She had done the first section perfectly but had received no credit for the second part, which she had also completed. While the professor was beginning some new lecture material, she asked why she had received such a low grade.

The professor said, "Read my comments. I don't remember your situation without looking at the test." Wei Ping still didn't understand why she had received no credit for the second part. She had answered all the questions, and she felt the professor was not being fair.

After class she again questioned the professor, who said, "My comments indicate you didn't follow directions. Instead of writing one-word answers, you were supposed to write a full paragraph for each question."

"I'm sorry. I didn't understand the directions. May I take the test again?"

"I'm sorry, Miss Liu, but the directions were clearly stated at the beginning of that section of the test," the professor explained. "I can't give you a second chance just because you're a foreign student."

B. The American director of the language center had asked one of the students, a young man from Korea, to come to the office because of his many absences from class. When Jae came into the office, he was not alone. An older Korean student came with him. The director was surprised because he knew that Jae, an advanced student, spoke English quite well.

"I'd like to speak with you about Jae," the older man said.

"Can't Jae answer for himself?" the puzzled director replied.

"Yes, but it's better if I talk to you first."

C. Professor Jones was in his small office talking on the telephone to his wife. The door to the office was open as it always was. Saeed needed to discuss a writing assignment with his instructor before his next class began in 10 minutes.

"Mr. Jones," Saeed said as he stepped inside the office. "I need to ask you a question about the homework."

Professor Jones put his hand over the telephone mouthpiece and said in an angry voice, "Can't you see I'm talking on the telephone? Wait outside, please." He closed the door as soon as Saeed had stepped outside the office.

D. "It's going to be a really tough test in computer class," Lee said to his friend Omar. "I've studied for days but I still don't know everything. Would you sit next to me in case I need help?"

"OK, I can do that, Lee. I've had a computer class in my country before, so it's not too hard for me."

During the test Omar turned his paper so Lee could see it when he needed to. When the test was over and the two friends were leaving the classroom, the instructor stopped them.

"What do you two think you were doing in there?" he asked angrily.

"Nothing, sir. We didn't do anything wrong," Omar said.

"I saw you cheating and I plan to give you an F on the test. I may even consider having you dropped from the class."

EXERCISE 3: TEACHERS NEED TEACHING, TOO!

Affective Purposes

To become sensitive to behavior that may be offensive in other cultures

To find ways to deal with embarrassing situations that result from a lack of cultural understanding

Linguistic Purposes

To practice listening to persons of other cultures

To express opinions clearly and with correct vocabulary

Levels   Intermediate to advanced

Group Size   Groups of 4–5 students each, of mixed cultures if possible

Materials   Critical Incidents handout for each student

Procedure   Same as for Exercises 1 and 2

Critical Incidents Handout

Instructions   After carefully reading each critical incident, discuss the following questions:

1. What cultural knowledge did the teacher need in this situation?
2. What did the student need to understand about American culture?
3. What could the teacher do to make the situation better?
4. What could the student do to make the situation better?

A. One of the English teachers asked Ahmed, a student who had become a close friend of her family, to play the oud, an Arab musical instrument, at the international dinner the school was planning. The student agreed, "Yes, I'd like to play at the dinner."

"Would $25 be OK?" the teacher asked.

"Twenty-five dollars? What for?"

"For being part of the program. That's what we're paying all the entertainers," she explained.

Ahmed was embarrassed and a little bit angry.

B. Claire, a new ESL teacher, enjoyed her classes very much but was becoming frustrated with her beginning grammar class. The class was almost evenly divided between two cultures and both groups of students asked questions of each other and talked in their own languages.

On Friday, Claire was trying to review for a test by asking each student a question: "José, please give me a sentence using the present continuous tense of *to be.*"

José turned to his friend, Samuel, and asked him the answer in Spanish. At the same time, Yoko and Naoki were discussing the answer in Japanese in the back row.

"Oh, now that's enough! All of you, just shut up!" Claire shouted.

The class became very quiet. Claire was embarrassed. Later two of the students complained to the director, "She shouldn't talk to us that way. It's not polite."

C. "Yoshi, can you give me the answer to question 5?" the reading teacher asked.

Yoshi kept his eyes on the book, studying the question. He was thinking carefully of what verb tense to use in his answer when the teacher moved on to the next student.

"Can you help Yoshi, Carolina?"

Carolina answered the question quickly although her grammar was not perfect.

Yoshi felt a bit uncomfortable because he knew the answer, too.

D. Although Mrs. Carter was new to the ESL field, she had taught in high school for more than 10 years. She loved her international students as if they were her own children. After helping two of her more advanced students, a young woman from Thailand and a young man from Saudi Arabia, to prepare for the TOEFL exam, she eagerly waited for the test results. When she discovered that both of them had gotten more than 520 on the test, she hurried to congratulate them.

The young woman, Chanjeera, was sitting in the library, head bent over her books, when Mrs. Carter found her. Patting her on the head, Mrs. Carter said, "Congratulations on your TOEFL score, Chanjeera."

"Thanks," Chanjeera said as she slid down further in her chair.

"Aren't you happy about the score?" Mrs. Carter asked.

"Yes . . . yes, thank you."

As she was leaving the library, Mrs. Carter recognized Ahmed in the long white robe and white head covering that he always wore on Fridays.

"Hi, Ahmed," she said. "I just heard about your TOEFL score. That was great!" She put her hand out to congratulate him, but Ahmed just smiled and stepped back a bit. "Thank you. I'm really glad I got a high score," he said.

EXERCISE 4: LET'S AGREE ON A SOLUTION

Affective Purposes
To develop cultural sensitivity

To experience consensual decision making

Linguistic Purposes
To practice the vocabulary of decision making (*I suggest . . .*, *Let's agree to . . .*, *Do you agree?* etc.)

To argue effectively for an opinion

Levels   Intermediate to advanced

Group Size   3–4 students each

Materials   Critical Incidents handout for each student

Procedure   Ask each group to discuss the three problems on the handout with the goal of finding one best solution to the problem. Tell them that the solution must be decided consensually; in other words, everyone in the group must agree that it is the best solution.

Give groups about 10 minutes to discuss each of the problems. Then ask each group to report its solutions to the class.

Critical Incidents Handout

A. You are the foreign student advisor at a large university. You have been directed to run an orientation of one week for new international students. The students who show up at the orientation are bored and hostile. They are there only because it is a required activity. They don't think they need to spend one week learning about American culture and university policies. What would you do, as foreign student advisor, to change their attitudes?

B. You are sharing a dormitory room with an American student. Although you have studied English for six months, you still have problems communicating. You are a serious student because you know that you must make a B average in order to keep your scholarship. Your roommate, however, seems to have come to college to play rather than study. She brings her friends into the room when you are studying, plays the stereo loudly until four in the morning, and frequently smokes marijuana in the room. You don't like any of these things, but you don't know what to do about them.

C. Your intermediate level ESL class just increased in size to 17 students. It seems to you that there are just too many students to allow the teacher to answer questions and to give you the attention that you need in order to progress to the next level. You go to the director to complain.

"I'm sorry," he explains, "we usually split classes when they reach 15 students but, at this point, we do not have another teacher and the college is so full that there isn't another room available."

"If it's going to stay this way, I think I want my money back so I can go to another school," you complain.

"I'm really sorry," the director says. "Next term will be different because the college won't be so crowded."

If you were the student, what would you do?

EXERCISE 5: THIS IS BUSINESS

Affective Purposes
To understand how culture affects business practices and relationships
To listen to and understand group members' opinions

Linguistic Purposes
To practice reading for comprehension
To use a wide range of vocabulary

Levels   Intermediate to advanced

Group Size   Groups of 3–4 students each

Materials   Critical Incident handout for each student

Procedure   Same as in Exercises 1 and 2.

Critical Incidents Handout

Instructions   After carefully reading each incident, discuss the following questions:

1. What problem has been created for the international businessperson?
2. What problem has been created for the American?
3. What cultural misunderstanding caused the problem?
4. How would you solve the problem if you were the international businessperson?
5. How would you solve the problem if you were the American businessperson?

A. Mr. Sakai was visiting in Chicago as the representative of a Japanese electronics company. Two American businessmen had made an appointment to meet him for lunch at an expensive downtown restaurant. After the three men had introduced themselves and had ordered their food, Mr. Johnson started the conversation.

"Is this the first time you've been in the United States?" he asked.

"No, it is the second time, but my first visit was to California," Mr. Sakai replied.

"Do you travel a lot in your job? I imagine it's difficult to leave your family frequently. You do have a family, don't you?"

"Yes, yes," Mr. Sakai nodded.

"Do you have children?" Mr. Carroll, the second American, asked.

Mr. Sakai paused. "Yes, yes, I have two children. My son is just finishing . . ."

Mr. Johnson interrupted, "Is your wife the typical good Japanese woman who stays home to care for you and the children?"

"Excuse me, gentlemen. I have your soup," interjected the waiter as he served the bowls of onion soup.

After Mr. Sakai had tasted the soup, Mr. Johnson said, "This is my favorite soup. I hope you like it. What do you think?"

Mr. Sakai seemed surprised at the question and looked blankly at Mr. Johnson.

"It's good, isn't it?" Mr. Johnson asked again.

Mr. Sakai seemed frustrated. He nodded and looked down at his bowl, hoping the conversation would end soon.

B. Mr. Smyth, the manager of an American oil company went to Saudi Arabia to negotiate for a very big contract. He had read about Saudi oil wealth and hoped to make a fast deal that would expand his business. During his first meeting with the assistant minister of petroleum, the American businessman was happy to find that the minister spoke excellent English although he had been educated in his own country. "Since his English is so good, we should be able to get right down to business," the American thought.

"Would you like some coffee, Mr. Smyth?" the minister asked.

"No thanks, I just had breakfast," Mr. Smyth replied.

"Are you certain you don't want to try our excellent Arab coffee?"

"Thanks, but I'm not much of a coffee drinker. Maybe we could just begin talking about dates of completion and costs," Mr. Smyth suggested, relaxing enough to cross one leg over the other. The minister looked surprised as the bottom of Mr. Smyth's shoe was pointed toward him.

"Since I don't have much time this morning, maybe you would like to return later in the week," the minister said.

C. Ms. Okada had just moved up to a management position in the sporting goods company where she had been employed since graduation from college in Tokyo. As part of her new assignment, the company decided to send her to Colorado to visit with retailers in ski areas in Vail and Aspen. She had studied English for many years in Japan but had never visited the United States, so she was quite excited.

She was met at the airport by Mr. Collins, owner of a chain of skiwear stores. "I'm so happy to meet you, Ms. Okada," said Mr. Collins as he reached out to shake her hand.

"I'm pleased to meet you, Mr. Collins," Ms. Okada replied keeping her hand behind her back and bowing slightly.

As the week progressed, she was introduced to many American businessmen and women, all of whom tried to shake hands with her. She felt very uncomfortable with the idea of touching hands and decided it was not important to adapt to this embarrassing American custom.

One of the top executives she had met commented after she had left, "I like the products that Okada's company produces, but she's rather a cold fish . . . a bit too formal for me."

EXERCISE 6: AMERICAN FAMILY LIFE

Affective Purposes

To become sensitive to cultural differences in family life

To develop creative solutions to ease cultural misunderstandings

To practice consensual decision making

Linguistic Purposes

To practice the vocabulary of decision making

To argue effectively for an opinion

Levels   Advanced beginning to advanced

Group Size   Groups of 3–4 students each

Materials   Critical Incidents handout for each student

Procedure   Ask each group to discuss the three problems on the handout with the goal of finding one best solution to the problem. Tell them that the solution must be decided consensually; in other words, everyone in the group must agree that it is the best solution.

Give groups about 10 minutes to discuss each of the problems. Then ask each group to report its solutions to the class.

Critical Incidents Handout

A. You are Mrs. Thomas, the mother of two children and a host mother for Maria, a 17-year-old student from Venezuela. When Maria comes to live at your house, you tell her about the only important family rule that you want her and your two children to follow. This rule is to let you know if she is going to be late for dinner, which is always at 6 or 6:30 p.m., or if she goes out with friends at night to give you a time that she will return.

The first week Maria is home on time every night for dinner, but on Monday of the second week you have prepared a special birthday dinner for your daughter, Jan. You think it will be fun for Maria to see what an American birthday party is like. The dinner is ready at 6 p.m., but Maria isn't home. You wait until 6:45 but are afraid the special roast beef will be too dry, so you ask everyone to begin eating. At 7:30, Maria comes home.

"Where were you, Maria? We were worried. Didn't you remember about the party?" you ask.

"I didn't think you'd eat. It's so early," Maria says.

You fix a special plate for her and the party continues. However, two days later, dinner is on the table at 6 and Maria doesn't return until 8:30. "I was studying with friends at school," she says.

The problem continues several weekends later when Maria does not come home on Saturday night. You are so worried that you call her school and even contact the police. When Maria arrives at noon on Sunday she says, "Oh, I was just having a party with my friends and decided to stay overnight." You are very angry and think about asking Maria to leave.

B. You have just moved in with an American family after living at home with your parents for 21 years. You pay the family the required amount for room and board. You are homesick and a bit confused about what is expected of you, but the family is very kind and asks you to go many places with them. They even help you with homework when you have questions.

As the weeks pass, you settle into a routine very much like being home in your own country. When you need a snack, you ask the host mother to prepare one. When your dirty clothes pile up on the floor at the end of the week, you ask the mother to wash them. One evening after dinner, everyone is carrying their dishes to the kitchen. "I'm going to my room to study for a test," you say.

"Just a minute, young man, I'm tired of you not helping with any of the chores in this house. Please carry your dishes to the kitchen and put them in the dishwasher."

You are surprised and hurt by her tone of voice.

C. You have been looking forward to a homestay in the United States for two years. "This will be the best way to learn English while I'm studying," you think.

When you arrive at the airport, a driver from the school takes you to the family, Mrs. Clarke and her daughter, 12 years old. Mrs. Clarke helps you to get settled. "I am a nurse and often work from 6 p.m. to 2 a.m.," she tells you. "But I'll leave your dinner in the refrigerator." During the first two weeks, you only sit down for dinner with the family three times. Each evening you try to practice your English with the 12-year-old when she is not busy talking on the telephone to her friends or watching TV.

You are frustrated. "Is this American family life?" you ask yourself.

Cultural Notes for Critical Incidents

Exercise 2B   Koreans studying at the same school frequently form their own "family hierarchy," by designating the older of the students as an advisor. The advisor acts as a go-between or negotiator when problems arise.

Exercise 3C   It is very common for Japanese to pause before speaking. In fact, not speaking immediately may be a way of showing respect for the person who has spoken or for the idea that has been stated. If the question asked is a personal one, and direct, the pause may be even longer as the Japanese person considers how to avoid a direct answer, which is a characteristic of the culture.

Exercise 3D   In Thai culture, touching the head of someone is a sign of disrespect and, some believe, may take away the spirit or soul of the person touched. For conservative Moslems, such as Ahmed, it is very inappropriate to shake hands with a woman.

Exercise 5A   The rapid-fire questions by Mr. Johnson and Mr. Carroll violate the conversational propriety of Mr. Sakai. "Speaking too much is associated in Japan with immaturity or a kind of empty headedness," according to John Condon, author of *With Respect to the Japanese: A Guide for Americans*.[1] Americans treat silence very differently from the Japanese. When an American asks a Japanese person a question, there is always a pause before the answer. When the question is direct, as in the case of Mr. Carroll and Mr. Johnson, there will be a longer pause while the Japanese tries to decide how to avoid a direct answer. When there is a pause after a question, Americans frequently assume that the question was not understood and attempt to rephrase it. This "additional verbalization is only likely to make the situation more difficult for the Japanese. Not only has the American asked two or more questions in the space appropriate for one, he has separated himself by not sharing in a thoughtful silence."[1]

Exercise 5B   Establishing a relationship with any visitor is extremely important in Arab culture. The chance to become acquainted slowly over a cup of tea or coffee is more important than getting right down to business. In addition, showing the sole of one's shoe by crossing one leg over the other is a serious breach of etiquette to the Arab.

Exercise 5C   In Japan, great attention is paid to relationships. The bow is an indicator of the relationship and can show, by its depth, who is older or of higher status. An American handshake does not indicate much about the relationship between two people. Additionally, for Ms. Okada, touching the hand of a man whom she has never met before probably seems very inappropriate.

ROLE PLAYS

Role plays work well with students of all levels. Beginning students are often self-conscious about trying to use the target language with appropriate gestures, accents, and inflections. However, if they are speaking in the role of a native speaker of the language, they are more able to take the risk. The emphasis is switched to total communication, both verbal and nonverbal.

There are two basic types of role plays: situational role plays and open-ended scenarios. In situational role plays, students are given brief descriptions of an everyday situation, such as moving to a new apartment and meeting a new neighbor. They are then assigned roles, such as the student who has just moved in or the neighbor who knocks on the door to welcome the student. Situation role plays can also be designed around problems or conflicts, with one person assuming the role of someone with a specific problem and another person assigned the part of the listener or advice-giver, or both parties can be involved in the same problem but each from a different perspective.

Open-ended scenarios are role plays that involve a series of student enactments centering around a problem. The problem takes the form of an open-ended story containing one clear, easily identifiable conflict, which is of relevance to the students. The story, which is usually read by the students, or told by the instructor, stops at the point of a dilemma. Discussion of solutions can take place at this juncture or roles can be assigned immediately and solutions enacted. The critical incidents described at the beginning of this chapter can serve as open-ended scenarios.

SITUATION ROLE PLAYS

EXERCISE 7: WHERE AM I?

Affective Purposes
    To put oneself in the role of a native speaker

    To experience an everyday situation that requires the use of the English language

    To build self-confidence

Linguistic Purposes
    To practice asking for and giving information

    To use the vocabulary of directions

    To use clear and specific words

Levels   Beginning to intermediate

Group Size   Dyads

Materials   Role cards

Procedure
    1. After students have had an appropriate grammar/vocabulary lesson regarding asking for and giving directions, tell them that you would like them to practice what they have learned by pretending to be people who need information in order to get to a specific place and people who give that information.
    2. Divide the group into dyads and give each person a role card. Students should not show their cards to each other. When dyads have had an opportunity to read their roles and ask questions about their roles, call each pair to the front of the classroom where they will enact their roles.

Role Cards

Situation 1:   A street in your city
Your role: A student asking directions

You have just taken a bus from your new apartment. You are looking for the First National Bank, where you wish to open an account. You see a kind-looking old woman who is selling flowers. Ask her for directions to the bank.

Situation 1:   A street in your city
Your role: An old woman selling flowers

A college student gets off the bus in front of the place where you sell flowers everyday. The student asks for directions to a bank. Give the student the directions he or she needs.

Situation 2:   A large department store
Your role: A businessman who is looking for a black leather briefcase with a lock

You need a new briefcase and would like one that is black leather. It must have a lock that cannot be opened by a key. Ask the salesperson for what you want.

Situation 2:   A large department store
Your role: A salesperson in the briefcase and billfold department

You are a salesperson who wants to win a trip to Las Vegas for selling the most merchandise this week. A businessman asks to buy something you do not have, but you try to sell him something else.

Situation 3:   A bus stop
Your role: The bus driver

You are a bus driver who is helpful and enjoys meeting new people. An international student who is new to town gets on your bus and needs help.

Situation 3:   A bus stop
Your role: An international student who is new to town

It is the end of your first day in the English language program, and you must take a bus home for the first time. You have been told that your bus is the Number 67, but you don't know how much money the bus costs and you don't know where to get off. Ask the bus driver for help.

Situation 4:   The hallway outside your English classroom
Your role: A student who is planning a party tomorrow night.

Invite your friend to a party tomorrow night at your house. Give your friend information about the time and place of the party.

Situation 4:   The hallway outside your English classroom
Your role: A student who is invited to your friend's party

A friend invites you to a party. Get specific directions to your friend's house from your house. Ask if you can bring something to eat or drink to the party.

Situation 5:   The car rental office at the airport
Your role: An international visitor

You have just arrived in Denver, where you have rented a car. You need directions to the Sheraton Hotel from the airport.

Situation 5:   The car rental office at the airport
Your role: A clerk in the office

You are new to your job and to the city, so when you are asked for information you will need to use a city map. You are very kind to the many foreign visitors who rent cars from you because you were once a foreign student in the United States.

Situation 6:   A telephone booth at the airport
Your role: A student who has just arrived in your city

You have just arrived at the airport in your city. A driver from the school was supposed to meet you, but you cannot find him. Call the director of the school and ask him/her what you should do.

Situation 6:   Your office in the language center
Your role: Director of the English language school

A student calls from the airport to tell you that the driver from the school was not there to meet him/her. Tell the student that you will pick him/her up in 30 minutes. Give instructions on where you will meet and what you look like.

EXERCISE 8: I'D LIKE A HAMBURGER

Affective Purposes
To make clear what you want

To activate the body and the mind

To try out new behaviors without risk

Linguistic Purposes
To play with the possibilities of language

To practice contractions

To practice questions and answers with *would*

To practice the simple present tense

Levels   Beginning to intermediate

Group Size   Groups of 2–3 persons each

Materials   Role cards

Procedure
1. After students have had a grammar/vocabulary lesson or a reading lesson that involves expressing wants and needs, tell them that you would like to give them a chance to practice the vocabulary and grammar points they have just studied.
2. Divide the class into groups of two or three depending upon the role play they are assigned. Give each person in the group a role card and allow enough time for them to read the card and ask questions. Students should not show cards to each other.
3. Groups then enact their roles in front of the class. Allow time after each role play for student comments or questions.

Role Cards

Situation 1:   A medium-priced restaurant
Your role: The waiter

Two students are seated at your table. Give them menus, take their orders (beverage, salad and type of dressing, main dish, dessert), and serve them politely. The restaurant is out of roast beef and steak.

Situation 1:   A medium-priced restaurant
Your role: A student who is having dinner with a friend

You are hungry and have been looking forward to having a nice roast beef dinner. Also, your friend took you to dinner last week, so you want to pay for the meal tonight.

Situation 1:   A medium-priced restaurant
Your role: A student who is having dinner with a friend

You haven't had lunch, so you are quite hungry. You want to order a steak, medium rare. Also, you are the one who invited your friend to dinner, so you want to pay for the meal.

Situation 2:   The front door of an apartment
Your role: A college student selling magazine subscriptions

You knock at the door of an apartment and try to sell the people who answer the door subscriptions to *Time*, *Newsweek*, *TV Guide*, or other magazines. If you can make this sale, you will be the top salesperson and will receive a college scholarship from your company.

Situation 2:   The front door of an apartment
Your role: The husband who lives in the apartment

You answer the door when you hear someone knock. It is a magazine salesperson. You always feel sorry for people selling things door-to-door, so you are very polite and interested in buying at least one subscription.

Situation 2:   The front door of an apartment
Your role: The wife who lives in the apartment

You hear your husband answer the door. It's a salesperson. Your husband is supposed to be helping you in the kitchen, and it makes you angry that he is wasting his time talking to the salesperson. Also, you hate to have salespeople knock at your door, and you never buy from them.

Situation 3:   The supermarket
Your role: A clerk in the bakery

You are busy putting donuts in the display case when a customer asks you a question.

Situation 3:   The supermarket
Your role: A customer

You are looking in the bakery for a specific kind of pastry from your country. You do not see it in the display case. Ask the clerk if she has this pastry. Describe it clearly, so she knows what it looks and tastes like.

Situation 3:   The supermarket
Your role: A customer

You are in a hurry to get to work and have to buy two dozen donuts. Another customer is taking too much time asking questions. You interrupt and ask the clerk for your donuts.

Situation 4:   The college library
Your role: The librarian

You are busy working on a computer list at your desk. A student asks you a question, but you do not hear him/her until the third time you are asked. Try to answer the question by giving specific directions. If students are too noisy, tell them to be quiet, so that they do not disturb other students.

Situation 4:   The college library
Your role: A student

You need to know where to find the newest *World Almanac*. You also need to know if you can check it out and take it home with you. Ask the librarian.

Situation 4:   The college library
Your role: A student

You notice a student standing by the librarian's desk. As you watch the student talk to the librarian, you realize that this is an old friend whom you haven't seen in years. You hurry up to the desk to greet your old friend in a loud voice.

OPEN-ENDED SCENARIOS

EXERCISE 9: I'VE GOT A PROBLEM

Affective Purposes
To develop sensitivity to the feelings of others

To create a comfortable atmosphere which promotes understanding

Linguistic Purposes
To repair communication lapses in your own and others' speech

To develop vocabulary

To elicit communication from all students

Levels High beginning to advanced

Group Size Groups of 3–4 persons each

Procedure
1. To integrate fully the open-ended scenario into your lesson, you may wish first to introduce the topic of the scenario, to present necessary new vocabulary, to read the scenario, and to follow that reading with a discussion of the problem and viewpoints of the various persons involved.
2. The next step is to choose students who relate to the particular roles to come to the front of the class to participate in the enactment.
3. You may wish to read the last paragraph of the scenario before students begin role-playing.
4. After the first enactment, other students may wish to try role-playing different solutions.
5. When all enactments of the situation are finished, students can be guided through a summary of the problem and the solutions presented.

6. Related follow-up activities include writing solutions to the problem presented or reading a related selection in a magazine or book.

Scenario 1   Ever since she was in junior high school, Anne has wanted to come to the United States to study English. Now that she is 17 and has finished high school, she believes that her parents should allow her to study for a year in the United States. Anne's mother, however, does not want her to leave home. She feels that Anne will lose a year of college by going to study English.

"I'm sorry, Anne, but I think you're too young to travel to a foreign country and to live there with people we do not know," her mother explains.

Anne replies, "But, Mother. . . ."

Scenario 2   When "Jack" (his American nickname) first arrived in the States, he asked to be placed with an American family. It is now the end of his second week with the Johnson family, and he is feeling very uncomfortable.

"I don't like the food and I'm not hungry at 5:30 when they eat dinner," Jack says to his friend Lee, who has lived with an American family for six months. Lee has heard that Mrs. Johnson is worried because Jack stays in his room all the time and sleeps.

When Lee sees Jack in the cafeteria, he says, "How are you doing, Jack?"

Jack pushes away his half-eaten lunch and says, "I'm. . . ."

Scenario 3   Maria's boyfriend, Tomas, and her mother come to the United States to visit her for a week because it has been more than a year since she left her country. While he is visiting, Tomas asks Maria to come home and marry him.

Maria's mother says, "You may never have the chance to marry such a nice, wealthy young man, Maria. Please say 'yes' to Tomas."

Maria, however, does not want to leave her studies in the United States. In three more years, she will have her degree in marketing and will be able to get a good job in her country.

"Your future is the question here, Maria," her mother says. "You must. . . ."

Scenario 4   Marios just started a new job as a night clerk at a 7-11 store. He likes the job but does not like Mary Ann, a woman about his age who has worked at the store for two years. Mary Ann never calls him by name; she always shouts, "Hey, you." She also tells him frequently to do things he has already done.

"I really need this job," Marios says, "but I don't know if I can stand to be treated like dirt much longer."

Scenario 5   Sami has been invited to a party with some new friends from school. When he gets to his friend George's house, he is surprised at how many people are at the party and how much liquor there is.

"Come on, Sami, have a drink," George says.

"Thanks, I'll just have a Pepsi," Sami says.

"Pepsi!" George laughs. "Here, have a beer or some whiskey. This is a *real* party, Sami, we don't have Pepsi."

"But I don't drink," Sami says in a quiet voice.

"You don't drink?" George shouts in amazement. "Oh, come on, Sami. . . ."

EXERCISE 10: WANTED: MARKETING MANAGER

Affective Purposes
To provide students with an experience in interviewing and being interviewed

To explore the dynamics of the interviewer-interviewee relationship

Linguistic Purposes
To practice oral questions and answers

To formulate written questions related to employment

To fill out a job application

Levels   Intermediate to advanced

Group Size   Four students per group (two interviewers and two job applicants)

Materials   Applicant role description sheet, interviewer role description sheet, job application, acceptance and rejection sheets

Procedure
1. Explain to students that they will be role-playing a job interview, with some of the students acting as company managers who interview job applicants and others acting as the persons applying for the job.
2. After forming groups of four in separate areas of the classroom, have students decide who will be the team of interviewers and who will be the job applicants.
3. Then have members of the group read the appropriate role description sheets.
4. Ask applicants to fill out the job application form, which they will bring with them to the interview, and instruct interviewers to meet together to formulate questions to use in the interview.

5. Have the two interviewers in each group sit together at a table or in chairs facing another chair in which the job applicant will sit. The interviewers then call the first applicant and proceed with the five-minute interview. The second job applicant should be seated, so that he or she cannot hear the interview.

6. After the first interview has been conducted, the marketing manager should ask for the second job applicant and proceed with the second interview.

7. Possible conclusions of the exercise include:

   a. Interviewers choose the applicant they think would best fill the position and then share with the class their reasons for the choice. (Applicants can be informed of the company's choice with the acceptance and rejection forms.)

   b. The class re-forms as a group to discuss the following:

      (1) How did you feel during the interview process? About being the interviewer? About being interviewed?

      (2) What types of questions and reactions helped people to feel relaxed and comfortable during the interview?

      (3) Which questions helped them to show their personalities? Which ones helped them to tell about their special skills?

      (4) What types of questions "turned off" the job applicant? What kinds of answers "turned off" the interviewers?

   c. Repeat the process with interviewers becoming job applicants and applicants becoming interviewers. Then choose conclusions (a) or (b) above to complete the role play.

Applicant Role Description Sheet

Background   Peak Performance is a sportswear company that has manufactured high-quality skiwear, warm-up suits, T-shirts, and sweatpants for 20 years. They are ranked third in the United States for volume of sales. "Peak Performance has not been in the international market, but recently we decided to try marketing our skiwear in Europe and Japan," explains President Paul Robertson.

The Current Situation   Paul Robertson is looking for a bright, energetic international marketing manager who is familiar with the ski industry in Japan and Europe. He wants someone with good cross-cultural skills and, possibly, a strong language background in either Japanese or French. A marketing degree or related degree is also an important qualification.

Your Role   You will play the role of a job applicant who wants a position as an international marketing manager with Peak Performance. This is a job you really want because it presents an opportunity to use all of your skills. Try to convince the team that interviews you that you are the best person for the job.

Interviewer Role Description Sheet

Background   Peak Performance is a sportswear company that has manufactured high-quality skiwear, warm-up suits, T-shirts, and sweatpants for 20 years. They are ranked third in the United States for volume of sales. "Peak Performance has never been in the international market, but recently we decided to try marketing our skiwear in Europe and Japan," explains President Paul Robertson.

The Current Situation   Paul Robertson is looking for a bright, energetic international marketing manager who is familiar with the ski industry in Japan and Europe. He wants someone with good cross-cultural skills and, possibly, a strong language background in either Japanese or French. A marketing degree or related degree also is an important qualification. He is willing to pay a high salary to the right person.

Your Roles   You will play the role of Peak Performance's U.S. marketing manager and his/her assistant. You have been asked by the president of the company to interview applicants who have applied for the position of international marketing manager. In the interview, you should try to

1. Discover skills of the applicant that would help him/her to accomplish the job.
2. Find out what type of personality the applicant has.
3. Keep the interview informal and relaxed.
4. Make the applicant want the job.

Write down some questions that you will ask each applicant to find out his or her skills and personality.

Marketing Manager Acceptance Sheet
PEAK PERFORMANCE SPORTING GOODS, INC.

Date _____

Dear _____:

It is with great pleasure that we inform you of our decision to hire you to work as the International Marketing Manager of Peak Performance, Inc. We look forward to working with you.

Sincerely,

Ned Danson
U.S. Marketing Manager

Marketing Manager Rejection Sheet
PEAK PERFORMANCE SPORTING GOODS, INC.

Date _____

Dear _____:

We regret to inform you that we are unable to offer you a position as International Marketing Manager. We will keep your application on file in the event that any other positions should be available in the near future.

Sincerely,

Ned Danson
U.S. Marketing Manager

NOTE

1. John Condon. *With Respect to the Japanese: A Guide for Americans.* Yarmouth, ME: Intercultural Press, 1984, p. 41.

6

Simulations

Although role play and simulation both involve taking on a role or "acting," there is a difference between the two activities. In role play, each student assumes a particular personality for an individual purpose; in simulation, the entire group is working through an imaginary situation as a social unit.

Simulation is further defined in adult training as "any integrated model which symbolically reenacts a real-life situation."[1] Trainers use simulations to provide an experimental setting, such as a business, a city council, or a school, in which trainees learn the dynamics, relationships, and roles involved in such systems.

For a student learning a language, a simulation provides the opportunity to assume the identity of a native speaker involved and interacting with other native speakers in a setting such as a family, a business, a school, or the government of a country. Not only does the student become involved and produce "natural language," but he also learns cultural behaviors that are appropriate to these particular social groups. Because simulations are experimental, they provide settings where alternative behaviors can be tested without risking the unwanted consequences of real-life situations.

EXERCISE 1: TO MOVE OR NOT TO MOVE

Affective Purposes
To practice coming to a consensus

To experience and become sensitive to differing opinions in a group

Linguistic Purposes
To practice the simple present tense in negative and positive forms

To practice the conditional form (*If . . . then*)

To use vocabulary related to expressing opinions (*I think . . ., I disagree . . .,* etc.)

Levels   High beginning to advanced

Group Size   Groups of four persons each

Materials   Role cards

Procedure
1. Explain to the class that they will form family groups in which each person has a specific role: mother, father, 17-year old son, and 11-year old daughter. They will discuss a decision facing the family. The father, Mr. Harris, has been offered a job in New York, at a salary double what he is making now. He has asked his family to help him decide whether or not to move.
2. After you have formed groups of four, give the participants role cards and instruct them to read their role and think for a few minutes about what they will say in the family discussion.
3. At a signal, have families begin discussing the problem with the goal of arriving at a decision that all eventually agree upon. Give groups 10–15 minutes to do this.
4. After each group has finished, have one member from each group report to the class on their decision. Debrief with the following questions:
   a. Was it difficult to play your role? Why?
   b. Would this discussion be different in your culture? Would children participate in such a decision? Would a wife participate?
   c. Was it difficult to reach a consensus decision? Why or why not?

Role Cards

Situation: Family must decide about moving to New York
Your Role: Mr. Harris, the father

You have been offered a job as manager of a computer sales firm in New York City. The job pays almost twice as much as the job you now have as manager of a small computer store. You think about how nice that extra money would be for your children's education, but you also realize that you like the job you now have because it offers security and the owner of the company is understanding and willing to raise your salary if business improves.

Situation: Family must decide about moving to New York
Your Role: Mrs. Harris, the mother

You have been teaching in elementary school in your city for 15 years. You love the children and the school situation. You don't want to leave this small town where you were born and where your children have lived all their lives. You have heard about the crime, traffic, and high cost of living in New York and don't think it's a good place to raise children.

Situation: Family must decide about moving to New York
Your Role: Kevin Harris, the 17-year-old son

You are beginning your senior year in high school and say, "No way will I leave Central High!" You are on the football team and have a 3.9 grade point average in your classwork. You are hoping for a scholarship to an Eastern university, possibly one in New York or Boston. If you leave now, you probably won't have a chance to get the scholarship.

Situation: Family must decide about moving to New York
Your Role: Karen Harris, the 11-year-old daughter

Music is the center of your life. You have played the piano since you were four years old and also have taken singing lessons for six years. Your piano and voice teachers believe you are very talented, but they are worried that you will not receive the kind of instruction that your talent requires in your small town. You've always dreamed about studying in New York and would be willing to move.

EXERCISE 2: LET'S GO SHOPPING

Affective Purposes
To practice decision-making skills
To work together toward a goal

Linguistic Purposes
To use the vocabulary of food and shopping
To practice numbers, prices, and addition

Levels Beginning to intermediate

Group Size   Groups of three persons each

Materials   Grocery ad insert for each group

Procedure
   1. Tell the class that they are going to divide into groups of four committee members who will plan the menu for a party for the class. The party will last from 6 to 10 or 11 p.m., so it will be necessary to have enough food to keep hungry students happy. The group's task is to make a shopping list from the grocery ad that will be given to them. The list should include all items needed for the food at the party, but the total of the items should not be more than $50. (The total can be adjusted depending upon how many students are in the class.)
   2. Have committee leaders report back to the group on their menus and totals.

EXERCISE 3: CONVERSATION CIRCLE

Affective Purpose
   To experience feeling in control of a conversation

Linguistic Purposes
   To practice conversation openers

   To practice conversation transitions

   To practice conversation movers

   To practice conversation closers

Levels   Intermediate to advanced

Group Size   Groups of 5–7 persons each

Materials   A 3″ × 5″ card for each participant with a topic from the Conversation Circle subject list written on the card, Conversation Circle skills sheets, and pencils

Procedure   Before participating in this simulation, the class should spend time discussing the Conversation Circle skills sheet.
   After students have some background and vocabulary for the exercise, explain that this activity will give them a chance to practice their conversa-

tional skills. Distribute a Conversation Circle skills sheet, a pencil, and a subject card to each participant. Divide the class into groups (5–7 members each) and explain that during the next 20 minutes they should do the following:

1. Talk to other students but only about the topic noted on their subject card or about topics that have been introduced into the conversation by other students.
2. Practice each of the skills discussed in class at least once.
3. Keep group size constant throughout the activity. In other words, if one or two members of one group join a second group, one or two members of the second group should end their conversations soon thereafter to join another group.

As the facilitator you should answer questions of participants and monitor the activity. Following the activity, discuss these questions with the class.

1. Which of the conversation skills did you practice? Which were easy? Which were difficult?
2. What useful words or ways of acting did you discover that helped make one or more of the skills work well?

Conversation Circle Skills Sheet

1. *Openers:* Ways of initiating a conversation or joining an on-going conversation. ("Excuse me, do you know about . . .," "May I add something to that idea?" etc.)
2. *Transitions:* Changing the topic of a conversation when you wish to do so or when you are bored, etc. ("Excuse me for changing the subject, but have you heard about . . .," "Could we talk about . . .," etc.)
3. *Movers:* Changing the content (participation level) of a conversation from one of the following levels to another: facts/thoughts/personal experiences/feelings/fantasies/jokes/etc.) ("According to this morning's news . . .," "I had the experience once of . . .," "Have you heard the funny story about . . .," etc.)
4. *Closers:* Ending a conversation and moving on. ("It's been nice talking to you," "I enjoyed visiting with you," "I'm afraid I have to move on. Nice talking to you," etc.)

Conversation Circle Subject List

Television	High school
Music	Restaurants
Movies	Books
Diet	Travel in United States
Basketball	Jeans
Baseball	Marriage
Soccer	Computers
Volleyball	Shoes
Family	Summer
Friend	Skiing
Test	Ocean
Singer	Teachers

EXERCISE 4: SPACE ALIENS, UNITE!

Affective Purposes

To increase awareness of cultural values and how these may differ among people and groups

To compare qualities and skills needed to lead a group with different values and traits

Linguistic Purposes

To practice specific physical description

To use the vocabulary related to religion, family, economy, politics, and roles of men and women

To practice the simple present tense for habits, customs

Levels   Intermediate to advanced

Group Size   Divide class into three groups (preferably male and female)

Materials   Newsprint, felt-tip markers, and tape for each group

Procedure
1. Divide the class into three groups: People from Alpha, people from Beta, and people from Gamma.
2. Give two sheets of newsprint, markers, and tape to each group. Explain that each group is a race of creatures from one of three planets: Alpha, Beta, or Gamma. On each planet all creatures are alike—they look alike and their religion and social class are alike; the only difference is that some are male and some are female. Each group will have 15 minutes to develop a description of its race on newsprint. On the chalkboard or on paper:
   a. Describe your physical appearance.
   b. Briefly describe your religion or spiritual/moral beliefs.
   c. Describe family life on your planet.
   d. Describe the economy of your society.
   e. Describe the political system.
   f. What is expected of males in your society?
   g. What is expected of females?
3. At the end of 15 minutes, each group is directed to choose one of its race to present a profile report to the other groups (3 minutes per group).
4. Following the reports, initiate a discussion of similarities and differences among the three races (10 minutes). Explain to the class that a war of the planets has destroyed Alpha, Beta, and Gamma and that the people who survived must begin a new life all living together on a new, previously uninhabited planet.
5. Redivide the students into three groups with approximately equal numbers of people from Alpha, Beta, and Gamma in each group. Give them a few minutes to get acquainted and to review their similarities and differences. Each group must then decide what type of person they need to lead their racially mixed group. Have the groups list the qualities of that leader on the second piece of newsprint. Ask each group to report on its discussion.

EXERCISE 5: EVACUATION

Affective Purposes
   To make value judgments concerning possessions in an emergency situation

   To establish priorities

Linguistic Purposes
   To put students into a realistic communication situation

   To bring students into contact with new vocabulary

Levels   High beginning to advanced

Group Size   Groups of 4–5 students each

Materials   Evacuation lists for each participant

Procedure
1. Divide the class into groups (4–5 members each). Tell students that they will pretend they are a family living in an area that is going to be struck by a hurricane. Their neighborhood must be evacuated to an area farther from the storm. Families will have just 15 minutes to get the things from their homes that they will need and to report to the shelter that has been set up in a local school. Each family includes a husband, a wife, a 6-month old baby, a 7-year old son, and a pet dog.
2. Give each participant a copy of the Evacuation list and ask that they individually rank the 15 things they would take in order of importance: 1 for the most important, 2 for the second most important, and so on through 15, the least important.
3. Group members then share their rankings with each other and defend the items they have chosen. Similarities may be noted in the top choices and these reported to the total group at the conclusion of the exercise. Since individual values are involved, no correct answers are given for this exercise; however, guidance on the subject of emergency supplies is provided in a number of Civil Defense publications, that may be obtained from the Department of Defense, Office of Civil Defense, Training & Education, U.S. Office of Civil Defense, The Pentagon, Washington, DC 20310.

Evacuation List

A hurricane warning has been announced on radio and television. Your neighborhood must be evacuated to a school located farther away from the storm. You and your family have just 15 minutes to get the things you need and report to the school. Listed below are some things you might think about taking with you to the shelter. Please rank the 15 most important items in the order of their importance: 1 for most important, two for second most important, and so on.

Special medicines   Blankets
Canned food   Soap and towels

Important family documents and jewelry

The family dog

Diapers for the baby

Transistor radio

Baby food

Changes of clothing

Toothbrushes

Coats

Portable TV set

Pet food

Water dish for dog

Games and books

First aid kit

Electric razor

Flashlight

Cosmetics

Hair dryer

Tool kit

Cooking utensils

School books

Outdoor cooking stove

Razor and shaving cream

Pillows

EXERCISE 6: I'D LIKE TO PRESENT YOUR NEXT PRESIDENT

Affective Purposes

To give each participant an opportunity to influence other members of his or her group

To develop confidence in speaking before an audience

Linguistic Purposes

To practice vocabulary related to description of personality and character traits

To practice all verb tenses

To use the vocabulary of persuasion

Levels Intermediate to advanced

Group Size Groups of 6–8 persons each, half of which are campaign managers, the other half candidates for President

Materials Blank paper and pencils for interviewers

Procedure
1. After groups have been formed, tell participants that each group represents an International Club on the campus of a college. The International Club sponsors many activities on the campus: foreign

films, International Day, lectures about countries, and so on. It is their task to choose a president of the International Club.
2. Have groups decide which members will be candidates and which will be campaign managers.
3. Then ask each campaign manager to interview a candidate to find out his or her experience, major interests, and personality traits that would make him or her a good president. The campaign manager should take notes in preparation for a two-minute speech that he or she will make for the candidate.

EXERCISE 7: YOU BE THE TEACHER

Affective Purposes
To allow students to experience the role of teacher

To participate as a group in a creative solution to a problem

Linguistic Purposes
To gain new insight into specific grammar problems

To practice the skills of explaining clearly and giving examples

To practice answering questions

Levels   Beginning to advanced

Group Size   Groups of 2–3 students each

Materials   Felt-tip markers, newsprint, a list of grammar points

Procedure
1. After dividing students into groups, tell them that they are going to be teachers of grammar. Explain that students have had difficulty learning some specific grammar points and that they, "the teachers," must try to figure out some new ways of explaining and illustrating these grammar points.
2. Give each group one of the grammar points. They will meet together for 15–20 minutes to decide how to present the information about the grammar point and how to illustrate it or give examples of it. Groups may use the pens and paper, may act out situations that use the grammar, or may use any other means of explaining it. The teacher should circulate among the groups to answer questions.
3. When each group is ready, have them come before the class to present their lessons. Give other students an opportunity to ask questions at the end of each presentation.

EXERCISE 8: INTERNATIONAL TRADE

Affective Purposes
To experience inter- and intragroup competition

To experience the consequences of conflict between group goals and individual goals

To identify how group and individual strategies affect the group's attainment of a goal

Linguistic Purposes
To practice following specific instructions

To practice asking questions and giving responses (*May I have . . ., Do you have . . .*, etc.)

Levels   Intermediate to advanced

Group Size   Equal-sized groups of at least five members each

Materials   Each participant should have the following: an International Trade rule sheet; an International Trade score sheet; one set of five Trading Cards (one each of yellow, green, pink, blue, and white index cards or equal-sized pieces of construction paper), in a large envelope; a name tag containing the name or geometric symbol of the participant's group; newsprint; and a felt-tip marker

Procedure
1. Tell participants that they are going to become powerful traders in an international market. Divide them into two to four equal-sized groups of at least five persons each. Give each member a large envelope containing five Trading Cards of different colors and a name tag marked with the name or symbol of his or her group. Instruct members to wear tags on their chests.
2. Give each participant a copy of the Trading Cards rule sheet. Go over the rules and explain that there are two kinds of winners, an individual winner and a group winner. The individual winner is the person or persons whose cards have the highest point value at the end of the final round of play. The group with the highest total of individual scores at the end of the final round of play is the group winner.
3. Give a copy of the Trading Cards score sheet to each group.
4. Announce the beginning of the first of six rounds of trading (five minutes). Group members may trade with members of any other group but not with their own.
5. At the end of the round, announce a five-minute period to add up the scores.

6. Conduct five more rounds with a scoring period after each round. In addition to scoring in rounds 2 and 3, suggest that teams plan strategies for gaining more points in the next round.
7. At the end of the final round, the teams' final totals are tabulated. Each team reports its total score, its individual high score, and the name of the team's individual winner. These are listed on newsprint by the instructor.
8. The following questions may be discussed:
   a. How did you feel about this trading experience?
   b. Were you trading for yourself or your group? Why?
   c. How did you decide who you would trade with and what you would trade?
   d. What grammatical structures did you use when trading?

International Trade Rule Sheet

Follow these rules for each round of trading:

1. Each trading round lasts five minutes.
2. Participants who wish to bargain must bow their heads twice before speaking.
3. Once players bow, a legal trade must be made; in other words, two cards of different colors must be traded. (Only one-card-for-one-card trades are legal.)
4. If a player does not wish to trade, this is indicated by folding arms across the chest.
5. A player may not show his or her cards to anyone, with the exception of the one card he or she is trading to another player.

Scoring At the end of each round, each team gathers to add up its individual and team scores. The score is the total number of points for the cards actually held by each player.

Yellow Card:	50 points
Green Card:	25 points
Pink Card:	15 points
Blue Card:	10 points
White Card:	5 points

In addition, bonus points are awarded for holding three or more cards of the same color.

Three cards of same color: 10 points
Four cards of same color: 20 points
Five cards of same color: 30 points

For example, the score of a hand of three pink cards and two yellow cards is 140 points:

3 pinks @ 15:	45
2 yellows @ 50:	100
Bonus:	10
Total:	155

International Trade Score Sheet

Group Symbol _____

Individual Members	Rounds					
	I	II	III	IV	V	VI
1						
2						
3						
4						
5						
Totals						

EXERCISE 9: WORLD CITIZEN AWARD

Affective Purposes
To make choices concerning one's own values

To participate in problem-solving as part of a group

To assess common values in a group and the impact of this on group decisions

Linguistic
To practice the vocabulary of decision-making

To practice comparatives and superlatives

Levels   Advanced beginning to advanced

Group Size   Groups of 4–6 participants each

Materials   newsprint and felt-tip markers

Procedure
1. After forming groups, tell students that they will participate in an exercise that involves making choices based on their values. Give each person a copy of the World Citizen Description.
2. Read the World Citizen Description aloud and give students the opportunity to ask questions about vocabulary or facts in the reading.
3. Instruct students to spend five minutes individually deciding on one person who qualifies for this award. Have them make notes on the reasons why they would support this person as a nominee for the award.
4. In their groups, ask students to discuss their choices. Have the group make a first, second, and third choice of persons they would like to nominate for this award. Allow 15–20 minutes for discussion and recording of choices on the newsprint.
5. Assemble the students as a total group. Post newsprint choice sheets in front of the group. The following questions may be discussed:
   a. What choices did all groups have in common? Why?
   b. How did your personal choices compare with the group's choices?
   c. How do the choices reflect your personal values?
   d. How do the choices reflect your cultural values?
   e. In other decision-making situations, do your values influence the choices you make?

World Citizen Description

The World Citizen Award was created in 1989 to honor a man or woman whose life has been dedicated not just to the people of his or her own country but also to human beings throughout the world. The World Citizen should have achieved renown in a particular field, such as medical research, science, music, art, writing, sports, or national leadership. However, the achievements in this area should have been made for the benefit of all people, not just for power or personal gain. Mother Theresa received the first award in 1989.

Each year a special committee of international leaders meets to nominate candidates for this award. You are a member of this committee and must responsibly decide on the three candidates to be nominated. After the nominations are made, information will be collected about the nominees and, at a meeting in two months, a final decision will be made.

The World Citizen Award is presented at the United Nations each December. The winner of the award receives a $500,000 grant to be given to the charity of his or her choice.

EXERCISE 10: LOST AT SEA

Affective Purposes
To experience consensual decision making

To explore one's personal and cultural values

To experience differing opinions in a group

Linguistic Purposes
To use the vocabulary of opinions (*I think* . . ., *I believe* . . ., *I don't agree* . . ., etc.)

To learn new vocabulary

To read for inferences

Levels   Intermediate to advanced

Group Size   Groups of 4–6 students each

Materials   Lost at Sea individual worksheet, Lost at Sea group worksheet, Lost at Sea answer sheet

Procedure
1. Distribute a copy of the Lost at Sea individual worksheet to each student. Read aloud the story and pause for questions about vocabulary or facts.
2. Then review the list of items, explaining any needed vocabulary. Direct students to spend 5–10 minutes rank-ordering the items.
3. Next divide students into groups and give one Lost at Sea group worksheet to each group. Tell them to discuss their personal choices with the purpose of arriving at a group choice, or consensual decision. Emphasize that each member of the group should partially agree with the group choices to establish consensus, but that they are not to use voting or averaging or other techniques to arrive at a decision. Groups will have 20–30 minutes to arrive at their decision.

4. Reassemble the class and briefly share decisions made on the first five items. Distribute, read, and discuss the Lost at Sea answer sheet.

Lost at Sea Individual Worksheet

Instructions You are lost at sea on a private yacht in the South Pacific. A fire in the engine room has destroyed much of the boat and its contents. It is now slowly sinking. You are not sure exactly where you are because important navigational equipment has been destroyed. Your best guess is that you are about 1,000 miles south-southwest of the nearest land.

Below is a list of 15 items left undamaged on the boat. In addition to these things, you have a good rubber life raft with large oars. The raft will carry yourself, the crew, and all the items listed below. The total contents of all the survivors' pockets are a package of cigarettes, several books of matches, and five one-dollar bills.

Your task is to rank the fifteen items below in terms of their importance to your survival. Place the number 1 by the most important item, the number 2 by the second most important, and so on through number 15, the least important.

_____ Sextant (a navigational instrument)

_____ Shaving mirror

_____ Five-gallon can of water

_____ Mosquito netting

_____ One case of U.S. Army C rations

_____ Maps of the Pacific Ocean

_____ Seat cushion (flotation device approved by Coast Guard)

_____ Two-gallon can of oil-gas mixture

_____ Small transistor radio

_____ Shark repellant

_____ Twenty square feet of white plastic

_____ One quart of whiskey

_____ Fifteen feet of nylon rope

_____ Two boxes of chocolate bars

_____ Fishing kit

Lost at Sea Group Worksheet

Instructions: This is an exercise in group decision making. Your group is to use the consensus method in reaching its decision. This means that you must agree upon each item before it becomes part of the group decision. Consensus is difficult to reach. Therefore, not every choice will meet with everyone's complete approval. As a group, try to make each ranking one with which all group members can at least partially agree.

_____ Sextant

_____ Shaving mirror

_____ Five-gallon can of water

_____ Mosquito netting

_____ One case of U.S. Army C rations

_____ Maps of the Pacific Ocean

_____ Seat cushion (flotation device approved by the Coast Guard)

_____ Two-gallon can of oil-gas mixture

_____ Small transistor radios

_____ Shark repellent

_____ Twenty square feet of white plastic

_____ One quart of whiskey

_____ Fifteen feet of nylon rope

_____ Two boxes of chocolate bars

_____ Fishing kit

Lost at Sea Answer Sheet

According to the "experts," the basic supplies needed when a person is lost at sea are articles to attract attention and articles to aid survival until rescuers arrive. Articles for navigation are of little importance. Even if a small life raft were capable of reaching land, it would be impossible to store enough food and water to live on during that period of time. Therefore, of first importance are the shaving mirror and the two-gallon can of oil-gas mixture. These items could be used for signaling air-sea rescue teams. Of secondary importance are items such as water and food, for example, the case of Army C rations. Items are ranked below with brief explanations that tell the primary importance of each.

1. Shaving mirror. For signaling air-sea rescue teams.
2. Two-gallon can of oil-gas mixture. For signaling (the oil-gas mixture will float on the water and could be lit—outside the raft—with a dollar bill and a match).
3. Five-gallon can of water. Necessary for drinking.
4. One case of U.S. Army C rations. Provides basic food.
5. Twenty square feet of white plastic. Used to collect rain water, provide shelter.
6. Two boxes of chocolate bars. A reserve food supply.
7. Fishing kit. Ranked lower than candy bars because "one bird in the hand is worth two in the bush." You cannot be sure that you will catch any fish.
8. Fifteen feet of nylon rope. May be used to tie equipment together to prevent it from falling out of the raft.
9. Floating seat cushion. If someone fell overboard, it could function as a life preserver.
10. Shark repellent. To keep the sharks away.
11. One quart of whiskey. Contains enough alcohol to use as an antiseptic for any injuries; of little value otherwise because it will cause dehydration if drunk.
12. Small transistor radio. Of little value since there is no transmitter (unfortunately you are out of range of your favorite AM radio stations).
13. Maps of the Pacific Ocean. Worthless without additional navigational equipment. It does not really matter where you are but where the rescuers are.
14. Mosquito netting. There are no mosquitos in the middle of the Pacific.
15. Sextant. Without tables and a chronometer, this is relatively useless.

The reason for putting signaling devices above food and water is that without these devices there is almost no chance of being seen and rescued. Furthermore, most rescues happen during the first 36 hours, and one can survive without food and water during this period.

Note: Officers of the U.S. Merchant Marines ranked the fifteen items and provided the "correct" solution to the task.

Source   Adapted from J. William Pfeiffer and John E. Jones (eds.). *The 1975 Annual Handbook for Group Facilitators.* San Diego: University Associates, 1975, pp. 28–34. Used with permission.

EXERCISE 11: FOUR CULTURES

Affective Purposes

To explore the effects of cultural behaviors on others

To gain insight into cross-cultural encounters

To increase awareness of how cultural mannerisms and rituals are derived from cultural attitudes

Linguistic Purposes

To practice greetings and leave-takings

To practice phrases and vocabulary related to guest/host situations

Levels   Beginning to advanced

Group Size   Four groups of 4–8 members each

Materials   A copy of the Four Cultures instruction sheet and a trait description from the Four Cultures traits sheet to each group; a paper cup of raisins, peanuts, or small candy for each group; and newsprint on which is printed the schedule of visits for the groups, as follows:

Round 1:   Group 2 visits group 1

Group 4 visits group 3

Round 2:   Group 3 visits group 2

Group 1 visits group 4

Round 3:   Group 3 visits group 1

Group 4 visits group 2

Physical Setting   If possible, use separate rooms or a room large enough to provide each group with some privacy and with an area in which to entertain. Each area should have several chairs.

Procedure
1. Introduce the exercise as a chance to experience a visit to another culture and to practice words and phrases related to visiting in a home. Divide participants into four groups and assign each to a different area or a different room.
2. Distribute a copy of the Four Cultures instruction sheet and one of the four trait descriptions from the Four Cultures traits sheet (a different description to each group). Tell groups to read their sheets quietly and to keep their information within their groups. Circulate to each group to see if there are questions.
3. Tell each group that they will have 10 minutes to talk about and practice their six cultural activities.
4. When all groups have practiced, call time and give each group a paper cup full of raisins, peanuts, or small candy. Tell them that this food will be what is offered to each group of visitors. Post the schedule of visits and direct the groups to take two minutes to prepare for the first visit.
5. Announce the beginning of round 1. Assist groups in getting to the right "culture."
6. At the end of five minutes, suggest that time is almost up, so the guests should begin their goodbyes. At seven minutes, call time and direct members of each group to return to their area and discuss what they have found out about the culture they visited. During this time, refill the groups' paper cups.
7. Conduct rounds 2 and 3 in the same manner as round 1, allowing a few minutes for group discussion and refilling of the cups at the completion of each round.
8. When the groups' discussions in round 3 have been completed, announce that visiting groups are to "do in Rome as the Romans do" and adopt the customs of the groups they are visiting. Then announce the schedule for round 4: group 2 visits group 3 and group 4 visits group 1.
9. The entire group is gathered for discussion of the experience. The following questions may be included:

    a. What were the cultural traits of group 1? (Only members of other groups may answer this.) Group 2? Group 3? Group 4?
    b. How did it feel to play the member of another culture?
    c. How did it feel to visit a culture different than your own?
    d. What were some of the difficult things about dealing with members of another culture?

e. What were some of the most enjoyable parts of dealing with another culture?
f. How did it feel to become part of the other culture in round 4?
g. Which was more comfortable: the role your group had been assigned or becoming part of the other culture?
h. Which of the four cultures was most like your own?
i. Can you apply this exercise to your own experience in American culture? In what ways does it apply?

Four Cultures Instruction Sheet

Try to follow the steps listed below when you welcome visitors. Your group should decide on ways you can do each activity below so it fits the culture of your group. Talk as much as you wish and use any gestures that reflect your cultural traits.

1. Show that you are saying "hello" as your guests approach from a distance. (Wave your hand or use some other gesture that fits your culture.)
2. Give a close greeting to guests, such as a handshake, bow, etc.
3. Invite guests to come in or to come with you.
4. Invite guests to sit down (on the floor, a chair, etc.)
5. Invite guests to have something to eat.
6. See your guests to the door and say goodbye.

You will have time to talk about this and practice it in your group. When you visit another culture, you must also act out your cultural traits. In other words, at all times act as if you are a member of the culture to which you have been assigned.

Four Cultures Traits Sheet

Group 1   You are a superior, military, very organized people with a feeling that you are better than others around you. This shows in your gestures and speech. You like organization and you like things to be in the right places. When guests arrive, you take charge and, although you treat them well, you make sure that they do things *your* way.

Group 2 You are a gentle, shy people who allow others to lead. You are very graceful in the way you move and in your gestures. When guests arrive, you put them in a superior position and frequently apologize for your home, your furniture, your food, and the way you treat them.

Group 3 You are a very warm, friendly, expressive people with gestures and words that show how friendly you are. When guests arrive, you try hard to please them; in other words, you let them make choices about where to sit, when to eat, and what to eat.

Group 4 You have a very calm, relaxed outlook on life. You never hurry and are never very formal. When guests arrive, you informally greet them and let them sit where they wish. Whenever you get around to it, you serve them some food, but remember that hurrying is just not your culture.

EXERCISE 12: THE WAVONIANS

Affective Purposes

To become involved in a simulated society in which different values are encountered

To become aware of feelings that develop when encountering cultures different than your own

Linguistic Purposes

To read for inferences

To practice the vocabulary of feelings

To practice interpretation of verbal and nonverbal cues

Levels Intermediate to advanced

Group Size Unlimited (2 role players, 6–8 guests, observers)

Materials A copy of the Wavonian role description sheet for each player, newsprint, and felt-tip marker

Procedure

1. Choose two people, one male and one female, to act in a role play of a simulated culture. Each role player is given a copy of the Wavonian role description sheet. Tell role players that they are to express

themselves in actions, and words. Have role players leave the room to read and discuss their roles.

2. Ask for 6–8 volunteers to be "guests" in the simulated culture. Tell them that they will be visiting the home of a Wavonian couple and that they are to talk and participate in any way that they think is suitable. Answer any questions that the guests may have.

3. Discuss the role play with the remaining students, who are observers. Tell this group that they are to watch the role play carefully for any cultural traits that they think are demonstrated during this time.

4. Have role players come back into the room, where they are joined by the guests. Begin the role play.

5. After the role play has ended, have observers as a group take 10 minutes to list various cultural traits they think were demonstrated during the role play. List these traits on newsprint. Then ask the role players to explain, in Wavonian terms, each trait the group listed correctly.

6. Discuss the misunderstandings that occurred between groups with different value systems.

    a. Which traits listed were correct? Was your understanding of the reasons for these traits correct?

    b. Which traits listed were not correct? Why did you misunderstand these traits?

    c. What American values have been difficult for you to understand? Why?

    d. What values of your own culture are sometimes difficult for foreigners to understand? Why?

    e. What feelings do you experience when you are in a new culture and don't fully understand the reasons for people's behavior? (You may wish to discuss feelings of disgust, hostility, fear, or ethnocentrism.)

Wavonian Role Description Sheet

You are a member of the Wavonian culture. Here are some of the most important traits of your culture:

1. When greeting a guest, the Wavonian puts the thumb of his right hand on his ear and waves the remaining four fingers three times. When talking to each other, Wavonians stand rather far apart, approximately two feet between speakers. They also use their hands

a great deal when they talk, sometimes pointing to the people they are talking to. Also, when speaking of events in the past, they use their right hand to point over their right shoulder, and when speaking of the future, they use the same gesture of the right hand pointing forward.

2. Being second in the Wavonian culture is more important than being first because Wavonians see the world as filled with dangers and fears. Therefore, to be served second or to be greeted second simply means that you are being protected from possible danger. For example, if you are the second one to be served your food, you might well be saved from poisoning, or if you are the second one to exit through a door, you might be protected from an unknown enemy. Thus, males are always greeted and served first and females are served last.

3. Wavonian men ask many questions of other men. They show their interest by asking about jobs, school, hobbies, houses, cars, and so on. They do not feel it is polite, however, to ask questions of women. If a woman asks a man a question, they usually suggest that she talk to another woman in the room. For example, a Wavonian male might say, when asked what job he has, "My wife can tell you about that."

4. When saying goodbye to guests, Wavonians open their right hands and rotate them in a circular motion from the wrist.

Please show Wavonian customs in all your actions, including greeting your guests.

EXERCISE 13: PLANE CRASH

Affective Purposes
To explore choices involving values

To experience problem solving in a group

Linguistic Purposes
To use vocabulary related to decision making

To use the conditional form (*If . . . then*)

To practice the uses of all verb tenses

To read for inferences

Levels   Advanced beginning to advanced

Group Size   Groups of 4–6 persons each

Materials   A copy of Plane Crash description sheet for each participant

Procedure
1. Tell students that they are going to practice making decisions in a group. You may wish to say, "It is fairly easy for groups to make decisions when they are dealing with facts. In this activity, however, you will have to think about values. Values are those parts of life that are most important to people and to cultures, such as the family, religion, freedom, and the like. The task of your group will be to make decisions based upon your values."
2. Form groups and distribute copies of the Plane Crash description sheet. Give students time to read the information and ask questions as you circulate through the room.
3. Give groups 20-30 minutes to arrive at a consensual decision. Remind them that each member of the group should somewhat agree with the group choices to reach a consensus, but that they are not to use voting or averaging or other techniques to come to a decision.
4. When the time is up, bring the groups together to report on their decisions and their reasons.

Variations   (1) Role-playing can be incorporated into the simulation by having each survivor appear before the group. (2) Survivors could be ranked according to which one should be chosen first, second, and so on.

Plane Crash Description Sheet

A 737 airplane crashed in a snowstorm in the high Andes Mountains of Peru. Minutes after the crash, a fire began in the tail section of the airplane. A stewardess, who was not badly injured, put out the fire with an extinguisher and saved the lives of nine passengers who had not been killed by the impact of the crash. The stewardess and a young man, Pablo, helped the remaining eight passengers get out of the plane. They determined that all other passengers were dead.

As the survivors huddle together in the freezing snow under the wing of the airplane, they hear the sound of a helicopter. The helicopter pilot cannot land in the rocky area near the airplane, but he drops a rope with a note attached to it. The note reads:

"I'm sorry but my helicopter holds only five people in addition to myself. Please choose five of your group to be lifted by the rope and taken to the nearest village, which is two hours from here. A dangerous snowstorm is coming this way, so I do not know when I will be able to return to this area to pick up a second group."

You are a member of the group and must make your decision from the following information about the survivors:

Lisa   American, stewardess, age 24, unmarried. Lisa saved the other members of the group by putting out the fire in the tail section of the airplane.

Pablo   Brazilian, age 28, married with one child. He is one of the most famous soccer players in the world and helped his team members to win the World Cup last year.

Jim   American, businessman, age 45, married with four children, ranging in age from 2 to 14. He is vice president of an import-export company that illegally participates in drug trade between Latin America and Miami.

Deanna   American, wife of Jim (above). After graduation from college with a major in Spanish, Deanna decided not to work but to stay home to raise their four children. She does not know about her husband's illegal drug dealings.

John   American, priest, age 65. John has spent his life helping poor, hungry children without parents. He has organized and built 11 orphanages for street children of Brazil and travels between the United States and Brazil arranging adoptions for American parents.

Maria   Brazilian, 3-year-old child. Father John is taking Maria to the United States to be adopted by an American couple.

Pierre   French, a famous scientist, age 50. Pierre is very close to discovering a cure for AIDS. He is on his way to meet with another researcher to share his findings. His injuries from the accident include a broken arm.

Cora   Colombian, professor, 38 years old, divorced, the mother of two children, 8 and 10 years old. Cora has degrees from Colombian and American universities and also is a well-known writer of books about justice in Latin America. She has suffered a broken leg in the plane crash.

Marta   Peruvian, 18-year-old woman, pregnant with her first child. She is traveling to visit her father who is dying of cancer.

Khalid   Kuwaiti, international student, 20 years old, unmarried. Khalid is on scholarship from his country to study electrical engineering in the United States. He had just finished his English language study and went with his friend, Manuel, to visit Manuel's family in Venezuela.

You   Consider yourself as a member of the group.

EXERCISE 14: PEBBLES

Affective Purpose
   To practice creative problem solving

Linguistic Purposes
   To use the vocabulary of advice and suggestion

   To read for clues that will help solve a problem

Levels   Beginning to advanced

Group Size   Groups of 3–5 persons each

Materials   Pebbles story sheet

Procedure
   1. Explain to students that they are going to read a story that presents a problem. With their group, they will try to find a solution to the problem.
   2. Divide into groups and give a Pebbles story sheet to all students to read. Circulate among the groups to answer questions about vocabulary or content of the story.
   3. Instruct groups to discuss the questions on the sheet and to be prepared to share their solutions with the class.
   4. Call the total class together to discuss the three questions.

Pebbles Story Sheet

A long time ago, an owner of a small clothing shop in London *owed* a thousand pounds to a rich money lender. The money lender, who was old and ugly, wanted to marry the daughter of the shop owner. He said, "I will forget about the money you owe me if you will let me have your daughter."

"There is no way I will marry that man," the daughter said to her father.

"I'll never let you marry him, my sweet daughter," the father replied.

Since the mean money lender could not get the daughter in this way, he proposed that they let *fate* decide the matter. "I will put a black *pebble* and a white pebble into an empty money bag," he said with an evil smile. "Then your daughter can pick out one of the pebbles. If she chooses the black pebble, she will become my wife and your *debt* will be *canceled*. If she chooses the white pebble, she can stay with you and I still will cancel your debt. But if she refuses to pick a pebble, I will have you thrown into jail and she will starve."

After talking to his daughter, the shop owner agreed. The three of them went out into the garden of the *merchant's* house and were standing on a path covered with small pebbles. The money lender bent down to pick up the two pebbles. As he did so, the girl noticed that he picked up two black pebbles and put them into the money bag. "Now, my beauty, you pick out the pebble that will decide yours and your father's fate," he growled.

owe—must pay	debt—money that must be paid to someone
fate—destiny, spiritual power	cancel—not make you pay, erase
pebble—a small rock	merchant—business person

Instructions Imagine that you are standing on the path in the shop owner's garden.

1. What would you do if you were the poor girl?
2. How would your idea solve the problem?
3. How did you reach your solution?

Solution The girl put her hand into the money bag and took out a pebble. Without looking at it, she dropped it onto the path where there were many pebbles. "Oh, how clumsy of me," she said, "but never mind. If you look into the bag, you can tell which pebble I took by the color of the one that is left."

Because the pebble in the bag is black, it looks like she has taken out the white pebble. The money lender will not dare admit that he is dishonest. Thus, the story ends happily because the daughter does not have to marry the ugly old money lender and her father has had his debt canceled.

Source   Adapted from Edward de Bono, *New Think: The Use of Lateral Thinking in the Generation of New Ideas*. New York: Basic Books, 1967. © 1967 by Basic Books, Inc. Reprinted by permission of Basic Books, Inc., Publishers, New York.

NOTE

1. *A Trainer's Guide to Andragogy: Its Concepts, Experience and Application.* Washington, DC: U.S. Dept. of Health, Education and Welfare, 1973 (HCFA 73-05301), p. 147.

7

Adapting and Creating
Interactive Techniques

After you have tried several interactive techniques in your classroom, you will learn which ones work well with your individual students and with your particular approach to teaching. Experimenting with several techniques should trigger ideas for adapting or even creating your own.

LOOK FOR APPROPRIATE TIMES

Start looking for those "right times" to use the "right techniques." Are there grammar points that are difficult for students to grasp? Are there curriculum requirements that seem boring to your students? Do you find yourself engaging in too much teacher talk at certain times? Do your students need more practice with grammatical points, vocabulary, or idioms? Your answers to these questions should help you find the appropriate times for interactive techniques.

DETERMINE YOUR GOAL

Having clear goals in mind as you choose, adapt, or create a technique will provide necessary boundaries for the strategy. You should decide in what ways the activity will enhance the personal and linguistic development of your students.

A need which arose in an intermediate conversation class illustrates the principles of appropriate time and clear goal. "I don't know how to keep a conversation going. All I can do is answer questions," was a common concern of some of the Japanese students in this class. To address this need, the instructor had students make lists of conversation openers, transitions, movers, and closers (see p. 125); however, she hadn't yet thought of a way to have them practice these skills. In looking through a book of adult training exercises, the Conversation Circle idea was noted and then adapted to the specific goal for the class: practice of the four conversational skills. It stimulated the students to speak on various simple topics and it allowed them the opportunity to try initiating a topic, changing it, changing content, and closing a conversation. In addition, it was fun, and they wanted to repeat the activity.

Remember that interactive exercises should fit the lesson and the class purpose. They should not be gimmicks.

BE AWARE OF WHAT IS IMPORTANT TO YOUR STUDENTS

Always be on the lookout for ideas that come from your students' interests and needs. This requires a certain flexibility on the part of the teacher. A situation that illustrates this awareness occured in a class of wives of Arab students. When the instructor walked in the door of the classroom, she noticed Semeha, a young woman from Saudi Arabia, showing her wedding photos to the other wives who were clustered around her, excitedly laughing and chatting in Arabic. The instructor joined the group and changed the language to English; she also changed the lesson plan and asked Semeha to tell the group in English about her wedding party. While she spoke, necessary vocabulary was recorded on the chalkboard. Some of the women asked questions: "Where did you go on your [the instructor supplied 'honeymoon']?" and "What did you do on your honeymoon?" (much laughter ensued here). After the discussion, students were asked to write a paragraph describing Semeha's wedding. Semeha was so proud of the attention she received that she later asked for copies of all the paragraphs, so she could share them with her husband. If the instructor had not seized the moment in that classroom, the assignment would not have had the excitement and immediacy that it had at that particular time.

SUIT THE ACTIVITY TO THE CULTURES

Try to match the cultural makeup of the class to the type of activity. If your students are primarily from one culture, be certain that students will feel comfortable with the technique. For example, the activity with Arab wives, mentioned previously, would not have been appropriate if there had been men in the class because the women would have been prohibited from showing the photos and discussing marriage customs. For the most part, Moslem students will not want to participate in activities that include shaking hands with or otherwise touching members of the opposite sex. Some of the simulations, for example, suggest that students hug or shake hands; these would need to be adapted to fit the comfort level of Moslem students.

What about a class composed primarily of Japanese? Although Japanese students are not quick to respond to questions and do not often initiate speaking, one of their major goals is to get conversational practice. If an activity is fairly structured and clearly explained, including the linguistic purposes, Japanese students will appreciate the stimulus to converse. However, those activities that require expression of personal feelings may make Japanese students uncomfortable.

In general, the guideline for matching an activity to a particular group is based on the instructor's sensitivity to the cultural makeup of the group. Ask yourself if your students will feel comfortable with the activity. Does the exercise require any physical or verbal actions that are taboo in the culture? Are the directions for the activity clear enough that students will be able to follow them? Would it be better to have written directions to give security to those students whose reading ability is better than their listening skill? Have you explained to the group the language-related benefits of doing a certain activity? Do you plan to follow up the activity with a discussion of what has happened and a summary of what has been learned?

ENCOURAGE STUDENTS' CREATIVITY

After students have experienced a variety of interactive exercises, or even just one successful exercise, give them the chance to create an activity of their own. Three of the critical incidents in the exercise entitled "Teachers Need Teaching, Too!" (p. 99) were suggested and written by students who had engaged in discussing and analyzing other critical incidents. Not only did the creation of these incidents stimulate conversation, it also developed into a writing exercise that required consideration of audience, style, and appropriate use of conversation.

You might discover a perceived need in one of your classes and state that need as a problem to be solved creatively through the creation of an exercise. Let's say your students are required to learn test-taking skills and they find it rather boring. You might say to the class, "OK, we have to work on these test-taking skills. I know this isn't particularly interesting to you, but the skills are important to learn. So, the question is 'How can we practice the test-taking skills in an interesting way?'"

If you help students to recall some of the general categories of interactive techniques, this may stimulate them to develop a way to practice the needed test-taking skills. You might say, for instance, "Last week we did some role plays. Can you think of a way we could use role play to practice test-taking skills?" Students might suggest that they write role-plays based on their experience of stressful test situations. Role plays could be stopped and discussion held to develop ways of using test-taking skills to diffuse the stress. At any rate, if students have a feasible idea, help them to pursue it by assigning small groups to develop the idea and to supply specific guidelines.

KEEP A FILE OF SUCCESSFUL TECHNIQUES

As you adapt or create new interactive techniques, record the activity in a format similar to that used in this book. Add notes about the success or lack of success of the exercise, so that changes can be made the next time you use it. Then file the written exercise in two ways: according to the type of technique (role play, simulation, warm-up, etc.) and according to the linguistic purpose for which you designed the activity (to practice use of simple present tense, etc.). This cross-filing should allow you easy access to activities for various situations.

Remember that interactive techniques are not just for the benefit of your students. They are also fun and rewarding for you, the instructor. These techniques keep you in touch with students' thoughts, values, and needs and encourage you to grow along with your class.

Appendixes

Cross-References to Exercises

APPENDIX 1: LEVELS OF LANGUAGE AT WHICH EACH EXERCISE CAN BE USED*

Beginning		High Beginning		Intermediate	Advanced	
2:2	4:1	2:1	4:2	All exercises	2:1	2:13
2:3	4:2	2:2	4:3		2:3	2:14
2:8	4:3	2:3	4:4		2:4	2:15
2:10	4:4	2:6	4:5		2:5	2:16
2:11	4:5	2:7	4:7		2:6	2:17
2:12	4:7	2:8	4:8		2:8	2:18
2:13	4:8	2:10	4:10		2:9	2:19
2:14	4:10	2:11	4:11		2:10	3:1
2:16	4:11	2:12	4:13		2:11	3:2
2:17	4:13	2:13	4:14		2:12	
3:1	4:14	2:14	4:15			
3:7	4:15	2:16	5:1			
3:10	5:7	2:17	5:2			
3:11	6:2	2:18	5:3			
3:15	6:7	3:1	5:6			
3:16	6:11	3:5	5:7			
3:17	6:14	3:7	5:9			
		3:9	6:1			
		3:10	6:2			
		3:11	6:5			
		3:13	6:7			
		3:15	6:9			
		3:16	6:11			
		3:17	6:13			
		3:18	6:14			
		4:1				

*With adaptation, the majority of exercises can be used with all levels.

APPENDIX 2: PARTS OF SPEECH EMPHASIZED IN SPECIFIC EXERCISES

Nouns	Verbs	Adjectives	Comparative/ superlative	Prepositions of position
2:11	2:1	2:11	2:2	3:2
2:12	2:2	2:16	2:3	3:5
2:14	2:3	2:18	3:11	3:14
2:20		3:5	6:9	3:15
4:1		3:11		3:16
4:2		6:4		3:18
4:7		6:6		4:6
				4:15
				5:7

APPENDIX 3: TENSES, MOODS, AND SENTENCE FORMS EMPHASIZED IN SPECIFIC EXERCISES

Present tense	Past tense	Present perfect
4:1	2:1	2:2
5:7	2:15	2:20
5:8	2:17	
6:1	4:1	
6:4	4:14	

Future	Conditional	Modals
2:15	2:9	4:11
2:17	2:13	
	3:14	
	4:11	
	6:1	
	6:13	

Interrogative		Imperative
2:2	2:18	3:3
2:3	3:6	3:4
2:5	4:1	3:5
2:6	4:4	3:15
2:7	4:6	3:16
2:11	4:7	3:17
2:12	4:13	3:18
2:14	4:15	4:6
2:15	5:10	4:15
	6:3	

APPENDIX 4: VOCABULARY EMPHASIZED IN SPECIFIC EXERCISES

Chronological order	Feelings	Persuasion	Problem solving
2:2	2:13	6:6	4:6
2:3	5:9	6:13	5:4
3:1	6:12		5:9
3:2			6:5
			6:9
			6:10
			6:13
			6:14

Directions (vertical, horizontal, left, right, etc.)		Sizes, shapes	Greetings, leave-takings
2:16	3:16	3:5	6:11
3:3	3:18		
3:4	4:15		
3:5	4:16		
3:14	5:7		
3:15			

Polite refusals	Polite requests	Expressions of gratitude
2:6	4:9	4:4
5:8	4:12	6:3
	5:8	
	6:3	
	6:8	

Bargaining/ negotiating	Description of process	Numbers (cardinal, ordinal)
4:9	3:1	2:4
4:11	3:3	3:1
6:8	3:4	3:18
	4:6	6:2

Food, shopping	Conversation openers, transitions, movers, closers	College Subjects
6:2	6:3	3:17

APPENDIX 5: CONTENT EMPHASIZED IN SPECIFIC EXERCISES

Reading comprehension	Inferential reading	Reading for specific purpose	Symbols/ words
3:7	3:14	3:10	3:9
3:18	3:19	3:18	
3:19	6:10	3:19	
	6:11	6:14	
	6:12		
	6:13		

Outlining information	Idioms	Observation of details	Information gathering
3:8	3:9	3:10	2:5
		3:11	2:6
		3:19	2:7
			2:12
			2:18
			4:4
			6:2

Consensus	Getting acquainted		Cultural understanding		Review of specific skills
5:4	2:1	2:11	2:7	5:7	4:3
5:6	2:2	2:12	5:1	5:8	4:5
6:1	2:3	2:14	5:2	5:9	4:8
6:9	2:4	2:15	5:3	6:4	4:10
6:13	2:5	2:16	5:4	6:11	6:7
	2:6	2:17	5:5	6:12	
	2:7	2:18	5:6		
	2:8	2:19			
	2:9				

Non-verbal communication	Impromptu speeches	Using art to express oneself	Spelling
2:8	2:17	2:12	3:17
6:11	2:20	2:15	
	6:6		

Index